LIMITLESS
YOUNG ADULT VERSION

Limitless
Young Adult Version

You Can Experience the Freedom, Power
& Potential You Were Created For

By Aaron D. Davis

© 2016 by Aaron Davis. All rights reserved.

No part of this book may be reproduced in any written, electronic, recording, or photocopying form without written permission of the publisher or author. The exception would be in the case of brief quotations embodied in the critical articles or reviews and pages where permission is specifically granted by the publisher or author.

Although every precaution has been taken to verify the accuracy of the information contained herein, the author and publisher assume no responsibility for any errors or omissions. No liability is assumed for damages that may result from the use of information contained within.

Unless otherwise indicated, Scripture quotations are taken from the Holy Bible, New International Version®, NIV®. Copyright © 1973, 1978, 1984, 2011 by Biblica, Inc.® Used by permission of Zondervan. All rights reserved worldwide. www.zondervan.com. The "NIV" and "New International Version" are trademarks registered in the United States Patent and Trademark Office by Biblica, Inc.®

Scripture quotations marked NLT are taken from the *Holy Bible*, New Living Translation, copyright © 1996, 2004, 2007 by Tyndale House Foundation. Used by permission of Tyndale House Publishers, Inc., Carol Stream, Illinois 60188. All rights reserved.

Scripture quotations marked KJV are taken from the King James Version of the Bible. Public domain.

Scripture quotations marked NKJV are taken from the New King James Version®. Copyright © 1982 by Thomas Nelson. Used by permission. All rights reserved.

Scripture quotations marked MSG are taken from *The Message*. Copyright © by Eugene H. Peterson 1993, 1994, 1995, 1996, 2000, 2001, 2002. Used by permission of Tyndale House Publishers, Inc.

Scripture quotations marked AMP are taken from the Amplified® Bible, Copyright © 1954, 1958, 1962, 1964, 1965, 1987 by The Lockman Foundation. Used by permission. (www.Lockman.org)

Scripture quotations marked NASB are taken from New American Standard Bible®. Copyright © 1960, 1962, 1963, 1968, 1971, 1972, 1973, 1975, 1977, 1995 by The Lockman Foundation. Used by permission. (www.Lockman.org)

Scripture quotations marked TLB are taken from The Living Bible. Copyright © 1971. Used by permission of Tyndale House Publishers, Inc., Carol Stream, Illinois 60188.
All rights reserved.

Contents

Dedication ix
Endorsements xi
Preface xiii
Introduction xviii

Part I: Who Is God? 1
Chapter 1: God's Not Mad at You 1
Chapter 2: Balancing God's Will and Our Tragedy 5
Chapter 3: Believe the Lie or Embrace the Truth 9
Chapter 4: Diverted Focus 13
Chapter 5: Grace Is Truth 16
Chapter 6: Jesus Is the Truth 20
Chapter 7: Jesus Restored What Sin Destroyed 23

Part II: Who Am I? 27
Chapter 8: How You See Yourself Matters 28
Chapter 9: As a Man Thinks 33
Chapter 10: I Will Remember Their Sin No More 37
Chapter 11: No Condemnation 41
Chapter 12: Spirit, Soul, and Body 45
Chapter 13: God's Provision and the Wages of Sin 49
Chapter 14: You Are Who He Says You Are 53

Part III: Where Have I Been? 56

Chapter 15: Open Doors and Permission 58
Chapter 16: Open Doors Part II—Intrusion, Trespassing, and Invasion 62
Chapter 17: The Infection of Rejection.. 66
Chapter 18: Processing the Pain.. 70
Chapter 19: 100 Percent 74
Chapter 20: The Power of Words 79
Chapter 21: Curse Consciousness 84

Part IV: Where Am I Now? 91
Chapter 22: Punching Puppets.. 92
Chapter 23: Suit Up for Battle... 96
Chapter 24: You Don't Have to Walk in Fear Anymore 100
Chapter 25: Fruit Is a Byproduct 104
Chapter 26: What Happens in the Mind Will Happen in Time 108
Chapter 27: Forgive and Forget? 113
Chapter 28: Four Hundred Ninety 118

Part V: Where Am I Going? 121
Chapter 29: Teach Us to Pray 122
Chapter 30: Believe That You Shall Receive 126
Chapter 31: Kingdom Authority 130
Chapter 32: It's Already in You 134
Chapter 33: Keep on Knocking... 139
Chapter 34: The Power of a Declaration..................................... 143
Chapter 35: It Is Finished 148
Conclusion.. 153
About the Author 156

Dedication

Integrity, loyalty, and honor are foundational principles through which most of my life and relationships are governed. I hold these principles in high regard in myself, and I esteem them significantly in others. I'd like to dedicate this book to two honorable men who have had a profound impact on my life but are no longer with us today: Pastor Tim Smith and Pastor Paul Jim Miles. My life and every person reached through the ministry that God has called me to are a part of their legacies.

To Pastor Tim Smith:
PT, during my early teen years (and probably the most pivotal time in my life) when my friends were making decisions that proved to detrimentally influence much of their life afterward, I met you in Woodhaven, Michigan, and my life was changed for the better. Your bigger-than-life persona, smile, and the way you made people feel loved and accepted made you the world's best youth pastor. You showed me the love of Jesus in a way that was unique to you, and I will never forget the impact you had in that season of my life.

To Pastor Paul Jim Miles:
PJ, I have so many fond memories of you, the big guy who loved and laughed so huge. Any time I think of you I smile. To this day, an experience that I had with you at seventeen years old in Troy, Michigan, when you taught me about Jesus washing the disciples' feet is the single-most impacting lesson in humility that I have ever learned, and one that I reflect on often with tears. Thank you for

answering the call of God and investing so much of who you were into the lives of others. I am blessed to have been one of those who was touched by your life. God knew that your example would be one that would influence the rest of my years in ministry, and He placed me under your leadership so that I could learn to carry on the torch of love and joy that you modeled so well. I love you and I miss you.

I look forward to seeing you both again,

Aaron

Endorsements

      Most people do not discover how to break through the barriers that have been created by their negative life experiences, the lenses through which they view those experiences, or the strongholds often created by these events until decades into adulthood (if at all).

      With the release of the Limitless series, Aaron Davis has provided an invaluable resource for anyone who desires to be free from the bondage of strongholds and experience the fullness of becoming the champion that God created them to be. This version of *Limitless* for young adults will revolutionize your successes and create a solid foundation for your future. Freedom and victory are not a distant hope or unrealistic dream. The Bible says that those whom Jesus has set free are free indeed, and this book provides practical applications for experiencing that freedom and walking in the victory and authority that God always intended for you.

Danny Gokey
Artist, entertainer, author of *Hope in Front of Me*, and Founder of Sophia's Heart

      As a former US Navy SEAL, I cannot emphasize enough the importance of having your mind right before you enter the fight. The key to effective war fighting and owning the battle space is DISTRACTION. If you do not keep your thoughts on task, you are literally inviting defeat. Anyone who has ever fought for a living knows that if you can control the head of your enemy, either physically or mentally, your chance of victory exponentially increases (where your head goes, the body will follow).

We have an enemy that views us conversely as the enemy, and uses distraction techniques to take us off task, and create strongholds and repetitive cycles that work against the initial battle plan set in motion when Jesus came into your heart. In *Limitless*, Aaron Davis presents you with life-changing guidelines for overcoming self-defeating mindsets, effectively managing your thought life, experiencing victory over strongholds in your life, and living your dreams by becoming all that God created you to be.

Jeff Bramstedt
Former Navy SEAL
Founder Life of Valor Men's Ministry

Preface

On a recent trip, I had the opportunity to enjoy lunch with a mentor of mine at the Ritz Carleton in Dana Point California. As we sat 150 feet above the ocean at an outdoor café, my friend unexpectedly asked me, "Aaron, what drives you in ministry? What are you passionate about?"

I wasn't anticipating the question, but without missing a beat, without having to think about it, a single word shot out of my mouth before I even knew what I was saying. "Freedom!" He cocked his head and narrowed his eyes, and I could tell that my answer was not what he had expected to hear. The usual answers revolve around the subjects of grace, marketplace ministry, healing, salvation, missions, prisons, human trafficking, digging wells in Africa, pastoring . . . I needed to elaborate on what I meant.

My greatest passion in life is to see people experience the fullness of the freedom that Christ purchased for them and walk in the assuredness, confidence, and authority of who God created them to be—conquerors in every area of life and victorious over every attack of the enemy!

I went on to share with him that I'm convinced that anyone who has not directly and intentionally dealt with the strongholds in their life is dealing with and being influenced by those strongholds. I'm convinced of this because I've experienced it myself. I was the fifteen-year-old church kid kneeling beside his bed in tears praying that God would help me do what was right and pleasing to Him, struggling with lust, anger, and bouts of rage. And I was the thirty-year-old pastor still praying, crying, struggling, and being held back by the same issues I had when I was fifteen. Things would be good for a while, but just when I felt like I was about to get ahead, I would be hit with one of those same three battles that had limited my progress so many times before . . . And most of the time I lost the battle.

None of us are as free as Christ exampled and intended for us to be, and I'm convinced that the primary reasons for this lack of freedom that most experience revolve around five areas.

1. What we believe about who God is.
2. What we believe about who we are.
3. What we believe about where we have been.
4. What we believe about where we are now.
5. What we believe about where we are going.

What you believe is ultimately what you produce. Perception determines reception, and perception for most is reality!

Attacks that have been orchestrated by Satan (the enemy of your soul) ultimately influence your unconscious belief systems (which I refer to as *lenses*) and how you process each of these five areas. You find yourself living defeated because your lenses are confirming the legitimacy of your present reality, ultimately molding your belief systems and stifling your faith.

In essence, people become convinced in some capacity that they are helpless in overcoming (probably because they have tried and failed so many times) and subsequently they become what they believe.

From these events and how you process them, compromises, behavioral patterns, and unbiblical belief systems sneak in (often because you have believed a lie) and detrimental lifestyle habits that I have come to define as strongholds take root, develop, and often grow beyond your ability to control them.

These strongholds create a ceiling for your progress and most often are the things that hold you back or tear you down a level or two every time you start to get ahead.

Think about it: How many times has it been the same attack, the same bad decision, the same self-sabotaging event, the same stupid mistake, the same behavioral patterns that have hindered your progress or set you up to fail just when you were about to hit that next level of progress in your life? This is evidence of a stronghold residing in your life!

Aaron D. Davis

Most often, this stronghold (and the behavioral patterns related to it) is rooted in something that happened to you when you were younger, how you processed an event or sequence of events that you have experienced over the course of your lifetime, and what coping mechanisms you have adopted as a result of these events.

A stronghold is not just the outward behavior you exhibit, but the entire process of belief systems developed leading to the behaviors that you have often spent years developing, nurturing, accepting, and excusing. The reason it is so difficult to remove these strongholds is because the roots go deep, and we are often living out what we have come to accept or believe.

Years ago I bought a house that had a huge weed in the landscaping. The weed was as tall as the bushes next to it. I went out there with a lawn mower and chopped that sucker down. It felt good. The ugly weed had been defeated! But a month later I noticed that stupid thing had grown back nearly as tall as it was before. So I sprayed it with weed killer (because that's supposed to kill it, right?). But it didn't work. Some of the leaves died and it got discolored, but it came back just like before.

It was obvious that this thing had been growing there for a long time and it was in no hurry to go away. I figured that because I hadn't dug up the roots, it was able to quickly reestablish itself, and I assumed that I could just pull the whole thing up (roots and all) with little effort. After all, *it was only a weed.*

Now, I'm a pretty big guy, and at that time I was a SWAT officer in the best shape of my life. I was in the gym every day. I reached down and grabbed that weed at the base and pulled as hard as I could. The weed didn't budge. I grabbed a shovel and began to dig around the weed. I wedged the shovel under the weed a few inches beneath the ground and began to try to pry up the weed . . . and I broke the shovel.

I was ticked off! I went to the garage and grabbed my pick axe. I spent the next fifteen minutes digging a couple of feet beneath the ground with the pick axe, breaking the roots that went in different directions and had even intertwined with the roots of the bushes next to it. I couldn't believe it. It was ridiculous—it was a stupid weed.

Preface

Eventually I uprooted the weed, but it took a lot of work and energy. The roots had gone down probably two feet into the ground. It wasn't a regular weed; that thing was a tree-weed! I didn't want to have to mess with that stuff again, so I paid particular attention to what it looked like.

Low and behold, a few weeks later, in the same general area, I saw a weed growing again and the leaves on it confirmed my suspicion—it was the same kind of weed that I had worked so hard to uproot a few weeks before. This time I reached down and completely uprooted it with two fingers.

A realization came to me in that moment as it pertains to strongholds in our lives. Most of us recognize that the stronghold is unwanted and ugly, like the weed. So, like I did, we grab the lawn mower and cut it down so that we don't have to live with the reality of looking at it all the time. But in a week, or a month, or six months, there we are having to face it again as it has reared its ugly head and messed up the landscape of our lives.

We decide that we want it to go away, so we pray about it and ask God to squirt it with some weed killer. And for a while that helps a bit. But the truth of the matter is, the thing got to the size it was to begin with because the ground of our lives proved to be fertile soil for it. So we realize that it's probably going to take some intentionality for us to uproot it. After all, in most cases, it got the way it did because we allowed it to grow, even though we knew it wasn't good for us.

So, like the weed, after allowing it to grow for years, we came to realize that uprooting it can be quite strenuous and difficult. We've broken some shovels, gotten tired of trying to pull it up, and many of us reached a point of just being okay with cutting it down every once in a while instead of doing what was necessary to completely uproot it.

But let me tell you, it is worth the work to uproot it. And once you go through the work of uprooting it, take the time to identify it for what it is, learn to recognize it in its early developmental stages, and do not allow it to remain in the soil again. You can keep it from limiting your potential and creating a ceiling in your life.

You don't have to live defeated! That ceiling was never intended by God to keep you from your destiny. There is freedom from the strongholds that your enemy has used to limit your progress. And in the coming chapters of this book, we will discuss the steps necessary to abolish the strongholds once and for all in your life.

Introduction

The Bible says in John 8:36, "If the Son makes you free, you will be free indeed" (NASB); Isaiah 53:4–5 says, "The fact is, it was our pains he carried—our disfigurements, all the things wrong with us. . . . It was our sins that did that to him, that ripped and tore and crushed him—our sins! He took the punishment, and that made us whole. Through his bruises we get healed" (MSG). Yet for many young adults in the body of Christ, these scriptures are a distant, hope-filled dream, an object to set your faith toward but far from an experienced reality because you don't feel free or made whole. You don't feel like Jesus is carrying your pains and all the other things that are wrong with you. On the contrary, it feels like *you* are carrying the weight of all your mistakes and sins on your own shoulders. In these circumstances, it's easy to become tired of fighting and losing the same battles, spiritually, mentally, physically, and emotionally, over and over again, and healing in these areas seems more like a wishful fantasy than a reality.

It's most certainly not for a lack of wanting to "do better," or praying that God would take away the sinful desire or help you overcome in these areas you've continued to fail. If tears and prayer were the only things necessary for overcoming, you would have experienced victory over these issues long ago. But after many prayers, many tears, and many repeated failures, you likely feel alone in dealing with the harsh reality that maybe you will just have to learn to live with this pain, weakness, and sin in your life—managing it rather than overcoming it. Maybe you think you will be able to deal with it for seasons, but never really experience freedom from the "free indeed" perspective that John 8:36 would seem to imply. All through my teen years and well into my adult life as a pastor, I too experienced this merry-go-round of success and failure, tears and prayers, temporary victories overshadowed by repetitive defeats.

As a pastor for over twenty years (I was a youth pastor for ten of those years), I have had the privilege of mentoring many teenagers and young adults. I can say without a doubt that the world today is completely different from the way it was when your parents or grandparents were your age. The temptations are different, societal acceptance of these temptations is different, and the ease of accessibility to fulfilling these temptations is different.

I know that your life is challenging and that you need the words in this book just as much, if not more, than the adults I have taught these principles to for years. Not long ago I was telling someone about *Limitless* and I said, "I wish I had known as a teenager what I know now regarding how Satan attacks and institutes strongholds in our lives, who God is as our Father and deliverer, and who we are as His children." As soon as the words left my lips, it was like God flicked me in the head, as if to say, "Make sure the next generation knows what you wish you had known."

Where Strongholds Begin

Strongholds most often begin when negative events take place in our childhood. Maybe you were like me and were exposed to sexuality before you even understood what it was. Maybe your parents divorced or one of them passed away, leaving you with a huge emotional void. Maybe you haven't ever really fit in with your peers because you don't feel smart enough, pretty enough, or athletic enough, and as a result you find yourself doing whatever you can to try to be accepted.

The truth is every young adult I have ever met has struggled with insecurities, and the reasons behind those insecurities are as vast as the numbers of people I talk to. Our enemy has attempted to mess up all of our lives at some point. That leaves us trying to figure out how to navigate those events to the best of our ability. But the truth of the matter is, most teenagers or young adults are dealing with this process with little support or input from parents or other adults who have been through similar circumstances. As a result, they do the best they can, but often find

Introduction

themselves asking a lot of internal questions while receiving very few answers that make the struggle any easier.

In these very vulnerable seasons, our enemy makes every attempt to worsen what has already happened with words he whispers into our mind. Do any of these thoughts below sound familiar?

It's all your fault.
You deserve this.
You're not good enough.
If you hadn't done what you did, that thing never would have happened.
You'll never be good enough.
You're a failure.
You're broken.
God doesn't care about you.

These are all lies! But it's hard not to believe these lies he's speaking because they feel like they are true. These lies are being planted in your mind with the intent of destroying you! The Devil knows that if you believe the lie, then you empower the liar, and he wants nothing more than to destroy you.

If you are like me, then you have tried to beat these lies by yourself. You've attended church services. You've asked God to help you do the right thing. You've prayed that He would take the sinful desires away from you. You have asked Him to help you defeat the areas where you have experienced repeated failure. Yet they are still there, and you assume something must be missing in you or that your situation must be worse than others because you still struggle with these things. I want to tell you something—everyone feels that way at some point! But the truth is you can experience more!

A Freedom Revolution

I'm convinced that there is limitless freedom to be experienced in these areas but most have simply not known it is available to them or have not been properly taught how to experience it. I believe a revolution is taking place. As the next generation of young people enter adulthood understanding who they are intended to be and what God has done to ensure they can experience the fullness He wants for them, the face of Christianity will change and victory will be the anthem of the body of Christ!

In this book we will address several essential aspects of experiencing the Freedom Revolution and abolishing strongholds in your life.

This book is divided into five parts.

Part 1: Who Is God?
Part 2: Who Am I?
Part 3: Where Have I Been?
Part 4: Where Am I Now?
Part 5: Where Am I Going?

As you read this book, you will see that each part is divided into seven chapters. My hope for this book is that it will be used as a five-week study where you could read a chapter a day (in less than five minutes) for five weeks, ultimately leading you to understanding and experiencing freedom in a way that you've never known in a little over a month. It can be used in a small-group setting or on an individual basis.

By the end of this five-week study, you will have come to an understanding of who God intended for you to be as a representative of His kingdom. You will understand what a stronghold is, be able to identify how it got there, and have the ability to address what gives it the authority to stay. By the end you will understand how you can be revolutionized by this freedom that Christ has provided for you. You will be able to walk in the authority over these areas of repetitive failure!

I've been a pastor of freedom ministries now for several years, and I love it. I love seeing Satan's hold over people's lives broken. I love seeing freedom and healing experienced after years of pain, frustration, and bondage. I love seeing the lights go on in people's eyes and faith ignited in their hearts as they realize that they no longer have to exist under the weight of the chains they've lived with for so long. Ultimately, I love seeing the kingdom of God trump every other kingdom or name that has tried to exalt itself above God's name.

Introduction

In all the years I've spent developing and teaching these materials, I've yet to see someone who genuinely applied the lessons fail to experience a significant and tangible change in their reality.

Freedom is no longer a distant hope for your life. It can be your reality! Even if you haven't experienced it yet, I believe you will.

The Bible says in Matthew 6:33, "But first and most importantly seek (aim at, strive after) His kingdom and His righteousness [His way of doing and being right—the attitude and character of God] and then every other thing that you need in life will be added to you."

I'm thrilled that you have chosen to read this book, and I'm confident that as you "seek first His way of doing and being right," you will not be disappointed. Get ready for a Freedom Revolution. The chains of yesterday are about to be broken. Your life is about to change forever!

For to us a child is born, to us a son is given,
and the government will be on his shoulders.
And he will be called Wonderful Counselor, Mighty God,
Everlasting Father, Prince of Peace.
Of the greatness of his government and peace
there will be no end.
He will reign on David's throne and over his kingdom,
establishing and upholding it with justice and righteousness
from that time on and forever.
The zeal of the Lord Almighty will accomplish this.
(Isaiah 9:6–7)

Part I

Who Is God?

If you ask a thousand people to tell you who God is, you will likely find a thousand different answers.

What I have found over many years of teaching this material is that *who* people believe God to be and how they came to that conclusion significantly impact how they approach Him. Many times these beliefs and experiences also impact whether or not they can even have a significant relationship with Him.

Some have been taught misinformation. Some have simply reached a place of inaccurate resolve based upon their personal experiences or on what they have observed in the lives of those whom they believed were supposed to represent God. But not all of it lines up with who the Bible explains that He is.

In Part I: Who Is God? we will break down the character of God from a biblical perspective and present a more consistent understanding of who God is and how He directly relates to you.

Chapter 1

God's Not Mad at You

More than any other thought that places people in a position of becoming bound by strongholds is the belief that God is unhappy with them. So many have heard, "God hates sin!" preached with such fervor that the natural progression of thought becomes, *If God hates sin, and I mess up all the time, and no matter how much I want to, I can't seem to get a grip on not sinning . . . then surely God is mad at me, displeased with me, or even hates me . . . because if I sin, then I am a sinner . . . or defined by that which God hates—sin!*

This line of thinking often causes people to develop a feeling of hopelessness as it pertains to pleasing God and adopt an "If you can't beat 'em, join 'em" mentality about sin. Many of us have done this, thinking, *If I'm going to displease God anyway, I might as well enjoy myself.*

Of course, afterward there comes the moment where you realize that you messed up and regret what you have done. Then you struggle with feelings of guilt or you worry about what people would think if they knew. This is when you come back to God and say, *I'm so sorry, I've done it again . . .* and you promise to try to do better next time. Only when "next time" comes along, you usually find yourself in that same place, frustrated, angry with yourself, and praying that God will help you never mess up again.

Then the racecar in your brain really takes off! Maybe you've sped down this road recently: *Because I mess up so frequently and God is angry with me, then everything bad that happens to me is a result of God's judgment against me.*

When you don't make the team, *God did it.*

When you fail the test that you studied so hard for, *It's God's fault.*

When your friend goes to doctor and they discover cancer, you think, *Wow! He must've really ticked off God!*

And in our minds, God is not the loving Father the Bible describes but rather the tyrant ruler of the universe who is looking for a reason to humble us into submitting to His way of doing things.

It's no wonder people don't want to serve "that God," but this is a gross misrepresentation of who God is. I'm absolutely convinced it is a demonic deception sold to people around the world in an attempt to keep them from a true and powerful relationship with the God of the universe who created man in His image to walk in power and authority over all the works of the Devil.

You're Not Too Young

To God there is no age requirement when it comes to kicking the Devil's butt! Many teens and young adults think that when they get older, have a family, or have entered their career they will be able to do more. But the truth is, God loves to use people of all ages. Don't believe me?

King David was still in his teens when he defeated Goliath.

Jeremiah was a teenager when God called him to be a prophet.

Daniel, Shadrach, Meshach, and Abednego were all teenagers when God used them to influence one of the most evil empires in human history.

And Mary, the mother of Jesus, was a teenager when she gave birth to Jesus.

God loves it when teens learn to do things His way and dominate the Devil long before they become adults!

The Devil will try to influence you when you are a teenager (and even younger) because he knows that the longer he can convince you to believe his lies, the harder it will be for you to succeed. So he starts on you when you are young, and he doesn't fight fair!

As a father myself, I cannot imagine anything more terrible than someone taking my son and torturing him. The only thing that would make that worse for me would be if somehow they deceived him into believing that I didn't love him and convinced him that what was happening to him was part of my will for him as his father.

I believe that this is exactly what Satan has done by capturing us with sin and then convincing us that God is mad at us, or that our pain is a part of God's wrath poured out toward us for sinning. Our enemy *hates* God! So how better to hurt Him than through His kids?

Why God Hates Sin

For the wages of sin is death;
but the gift of God is eternal life through Jesus Christ our Lord.
(Romans 6:23 KJV)

From a biblical perspective, it is undeniable that God hates sin, but I'm convinced it's not for the reason that most assume. What if God hates sin because He loves you more than you could possibly imagine? Is it possible that God hates sin, not because it hurts Him, but because sin produces death in your life? What if God hates sin because it hurts you and He loves you intensely? If this is true, how might this realization impact how you view sin, or even God?

The Bible says that God loves you, that every good and perfect gift comes from Him, and that He perfects that which concerns you (John 3:16, James 1:17, 1 Peter 5:7). (That means He cares about you and wants to help you fix what's broken, not strike you down for a lack of commitment.) He's a good God who wants to do good things for you. You are His child, and He adores you!

He loves you so much, and He wants you to know it. Understanding this love is the last thing our enemy (Satan) wants you to do because he knows that once you grasp how deeply and profoundly God loves you, the enemy's grip on your life will be significantly weakened.

God's not mad at you. He loves you! He's not upset with you. You are not a disappointment. He expects that as you grow in your relationship with Him you will make mistakes, and He has provided a way of victory *in spite of those mistakes*!

Take a deep breath, smile, and understand this: nothing you've done has surprised God, and there's nothing you can do to separate yourself from His endless love.

Now you are taking your first steps toward walking in the freedom and authority that you were created to exercise in this life.

Chapter 2

Balancing God's Will and Our Tragedy

Looking at God through the lenses of His intense love for us changes the way we process many perceptions of God. It also poses some very legitimate questions, such as: *If God is good and He loves us, why have some things happened the way they have?*

I've heard people say, "God gave me cancer to teach me to obey Him, and now that the tumor is gone I'm better for it." In their mind, it was all a part of God's master plan to punish them into submission and teach them a lesson in order for them to be better in the long run. But what about the other guy who died from the same type of tumor? What was his lesson? Was God *good* to one but *failed* the other?

It's hard to completely make sense of God from this perspective because what seems logical in one person's situation doesn't from the other person's. Then the common Christian and religious excuses and clichés for God are presented (I know I heard them as a teenager and young adult, and you probably have too) to explain our lack of understanding, like, "Well, God's ways are not our ways and we just won't understand until we get to the other side." Or, "God's plan was to use this death to bring more people to Him; after all, God works everything together for our good, so this must just be a part of His plan."

We can't make sense of this broken world, so in order to keep from losing faith we make excuses for what confuses us, and the easiest thing to blame is "God's will." But if we are honest, it doesn't give us total peace, and it doesn't really fit with the God of the Bible. So what if it's not the circumstances that don't make sense, but the lenses we are viewing them through? Let me paint a picture through a different set of lenses.

The Wages of Sin or the Will of God?

We live in a world plagued with sin, but it's possible that much of what we experience negatively in our lives is a direct result of the *wages of sin* and not necessarily the *will of God*. What if many of our experiences are a result of what happens when people choose to do things their way (sin's way) instead of God's way? What if a combination of our choices and our ignorance is producing a whole lot more of our negative experiences than God's will?

Here's an example of what I mean. In 1986, there was a nuclear power plant meltdown in the Ukraine known now as the Chernobyl disaster. The city of Pripyat was evacuated as a result and remains a ghost town to this day. Radiation has completely saturated the structures and even the soil of this region, and it is uninhabitable, unless, of course, you are okay with suffering the consequences of living there.

If you wandered into the abandoned city of Pripyat today, unaware of the dangers of invisible radiation upon the environment, you might assume that you had hit the jackpot of discovering your own abandoned city. But your ignorance would not protect you from the nuclear fallout of radiation silently impacting your body. In time, because of your proximity to it and emersion in it, the unseen radiation would have its effects upon you and eventually kill you.

The kingdom of sin has much the same effect upon our environment. The wages of sin still produce death and man's choices toward sin (which includes the choices of others) impact all of our realities.

I Choose to Do . . .

I remember a few years ago I was speaking with one of my teenaged students named Malachi who had been in repeated trouble with the law. I told him that he was at a crossroad in his life and that if he didn't make better decisions, the road he was on would ultimately lead him to prison for the rest of his life. Malachi looked at me and said, "Pastor Aaron, I know what's right and I know what's wrong. I choose to do what's wrong, and I wish you would shut up and quit telling me to do what's right."

A few months later I was visiting Malachi in prison as he was facing murder charges, and I reminded him of the day he told me to shut up and quit telling him to do what is right. He looked up at me, crying, and said, "Pastor Aaron, please pray for me." I prayed for him, but it was too late. He had made a decision that cost him his freedom for the next twenty-five years and cost some other people their lives. The people Malachi killed didn't deserve to die, but his choice to do what was wrong directly impacted their life.

Another example of how our choices can impact the innocent is when a pregnant mother chooses to do drugs. Every year 320,000 innocent babies are born addicted to drugs. Those babies had nothing to do with creating their addiction, but it does not diminish the fact that their mothers' choices directly impacted them.

Or what about the sixteen-year-old who went to a party, drank illegally, chose to drive home drunk, got in an accident, and killed a family of four coming home from the movies? That family did nothing wrong, but the teen's choice to drive drunk still directly impacted all those involved.

So many scenarios that we question like this, from a parent choosing to cheat on their spouse and breaking up the family, to starving children in Africa, to diseases that plague our bodies, are often directly related to poor and selfish choices people have made.

I've heard it said that the entire world could be fed on the food produced in Texas alone. But for reasons ranging from greed to simply not caring, choices are not being made to use the food in a way that could feed the world. And medical science has proven that many cancers and most instances of heart disease are a direct result of the food we place on the end of our fork or the chemicals we intentionally take into our bodies. But we still don't make wise choices about what we eat or consume.

For those who simply say, "It must just be God's will," I ask, what part was God's will in the examples above? Was it Malachi continuing to choose to do what's wrong? The mother putting drugs into her body and impacting her unborn baby? The teen drinking illegally? The teen choosing to drive while intoxicated? Or was it when the drunk teen crossed the median into oncoming traffic? What about when the innocent family was tragically killed? Are these really *God's will*? Or are these just the *fallout consequences* of someone's sinful choices?

What if God's will rests not in man's choice to sin and the fallout we all experience but rather in us becoming who were created to be? If we were created in the image of God (which we are) and seek His rule in our lives to the point where we can hear His voice and follow His leading to the fullest, we can lead a joyful, peaceful life that is honoring to God and we can impact our spheres of influences for good. Maybe we can even avoid the tragedy a few miles up the road.

I would never argue against God, in His faithfulness, working everything together for our good. He certainly has an amazing way of turning tragedy to triumph. But what if the reason He does it has little (if anything) to do with His participation (or will) in your tragedy, but rather because God, in His immense love for you, is not content to allow tragedy to be the last word in your life?

Chapter 3

Believe the Lie or Embrace the Truth

I've heard it said that we give the Devil credit for much more power than he actually has, and that his only real power rests in his ability to deceive us into using our God-given authority on the earth to establish the kingdom of sin. The Bible says that the thief (Satan) comes to steal, kill, and destroy, but that Christ came that we might experience life in this earth to the fullest extent (John 10:10).

Over and over throughout Scripture we see that Satan's intentions are clear. In Genesis 3, he deceived Adam and Eve in the garden. In Isaiah 14:16, he is the one that the world ponders, *Is this really the one who deceived the nations?* In Mark 4:15, he is the one who comes immediately to try to snatch the seed of truth planted in your life. In John 8:44, he is described as the one who has "no truth in him" and "the father of lies." In 2 Corinthians 11:14, he's the one who disguises himself as "an angel of light." And in 2 Timothy 2:26, he is the one who deceived man into being evil . . . and the list goes on. He is a deceiver!

The Devil Hates God

It becomes quickly apparent that the Devil hates God and he hates us too. We were created in God's image and likeness. We remind him of our Father, and he uses us to hurt God and to try to disrupt God's plan for His children by deceiving and perverting that which God created for greatness: you!

The Bible says that there is *no truth* in Satan. In other words, every time he opens his mouth and whispers something to you that is contrary to what God says about you, *it is a lie*! It is a deception intended to cause you to believe something about yourself or about how God feels about you that is completely false in order to distract you from the truth of who God is, who you are to God, and what He created you to be.

When you believe the lie, you empower the liar!

Have you ever loved someone younger than you like a little brother or sister? Or a niece, nephew, or cousin? The Bible says that God loves us more than any person could possibly love a child (Matthew 6:26-34), and if we know how to love children, how much more must our heavenly Father, who created us to love and is defined by love Himself, love us? The Bible says that "God is love" (1 John 4:8).

God is *at least* as loving of a father as I am. God is *at least* as compassionate toward people and their needs as you are. God is *at least* as caring about that which concerns His children as any loving person.

The Bible says that He gives good gifts to His children (Matthew 7:11). So what are some of those "good gifts"? He knows that you have many needs and that there will be hard times. He is your provider and promises to meet your needs and be there for you if you will allow Him into your circumstances and invite His intervention. He sees your feelings of insecurity so He becomes your confidence and biggest fan. He cries when you hurt and cheers when you win. He knows you will mess up and offers forgiveness, no condemnation, and a restored relationship—even paying for your sins before you ever commit them! He knows that there will be times when you will worry and He offers peace. The Bible says that He is the "Prince of Peace" (Isaiah 9:6) and that He will help you have a supernatural calming peace that can only come from Him (Philippians 4:7). He knows you will experience sadness and gives you His joy as your strength. He knows that sometimes you will lose your cool, that your emotions and sometimes your hormones will be raging, and He offers as a gift to you self-control that is not natural to our fallen state.

He realizes that sometimes people will be mean, hateful, and hurtful, and in those moments He gives you kindness, goodness, tolerance, and gentleness. He knows that people will be unloving and that you will feel unlovable at times (or that you will not know how to love in return), and in those moments His gift to you is love on a scale that you cannot understand but simply have to acknowledge and accept as an amazing aspect of who God is and who you can be in Him.

In the moments where you are weak or feeling distant from Him, it is God who fills the voids, covers the sins, forgets the wrongs, forgives the poor choices, and believes in us—even when you don't believe in yourself. Because, even though you might not have known or experienced this fully in the past, God knows how to give you the good gifts you want and need!

Don't Believe the Lie

It's not God who condemns us. It's not God who reminds us of our past. It's not God who points out our sin or makes us feel inadequate or unworthy because of the things we have done. That's our enemy doing that. Satan would like you to believe that God feels that way about you because as long as you believe you are not worthy to approach God, you won't. Reject those lies that contradict what the Bible says about you and how God feels about you.

When you believe the lie, you empower the liar, but the Bible says the truth is what will set you free (John 8:32). Will you believe and embrace that truth today? If it seems too much right now, will you at least consider the possibility that what you have read here may actually be presenting you with a truth that you've not yet understood? Perhaps now you can start on a journey of seeing yourself, and God, through new lenses.

The Bible says in Psalm 139:14 that you have been "wonderfully made." You are not a mistake. You are not broken. You are not even defined by the bad choices you may have made. You are loved and accepted by God. He thinks you are amazing, and He is looking forward to seeing you become all that He created you to be!

Close your eyes now and see Jesus smiling at you. Do you see His eyes? That's love in His eyes. He's not disappointed in you. He is proud beyond belief of you. And He's excited to see you fulfill your potential as you grow and discover the freedom and power that He has provided for you!

Chapter 4

Diverted Focus

One of the most effective ways that the Devil is able to deceive us is through diverted focus. If he can get us to take our eyes off of the truth of who God is, then it is much easier to convince us of alternative and less-perfect ideas of Him.

What we believe significantly affects how we respond. This is why the Devil is so intentional in his attempts to convince us to believe his lies. You'll hear me say it many times in this book: he knows that *when we believe the lie, we empower the liar*! And in turn, what we do is directly impacted by what we believe. You don't have to tell me what you believe—your actions show me! We live out what we believe in our daily choices. And oftentimes those beliefs have painful consequences.

Recently, my seven-year-old son, Rocky, entered a jiu-jitsu tournament. Before every tournament I have a conversation with him about remembering what he has learned and applying what he has practiced. I always tell him, "You are good enough to win every match today if you will keep your head in the match and do what you know to do." He is that good, but I know sometimes it's easy to look at your opposition and begin to doubt what you know is the truth, so I try to disarm that doubt before it has a chance to take root. Like all of us, though, sometimes that doubt still sneaks in and messes with him.

In the first round, Rocky was paired against another boy who was at least three inches taller than he was and a few years older. I could tell by his face as he stepped on the mat that he was already defeated in his mind. He didn't think he could win. The referee turned to the two boys and asked, "Do either of you have any questions?" My son, being the quick-witted kid that he is,

Diverted Focus

made the ref laugh when he said, "Don't you think he's a bit taller than me?" The referee gave the signal and the match began. Rocky trains four days a week in his sport. He was physically prepared for this tournament but performed far below his ability in this first match . . . and he lost.

Interestingly, Rocky still made it to the finals in his division, and guess who was there to face him for the gold medal? That's right, the *bigger kid* who'd already schooled him in the first round.

I hadn't had a pep talk with Rocky, and as far as I knew, nothing had changed, but when he stepped on the mat this time he carried a different confidence. He had a determined look in his eyes. And as his daddy, I grinned. My champion remembered who he was.

Even though the same two kids were on the mat, this final match was completely different from the first. Same kids, different competitors. This time Rocky was victorious, and not only did he win, but he shut out his opponent 7–0. That's right, the bigger kid didn't even score a point!

When Rocky stepped off the mat I asked him what happened. He smiled and said, "Daddy, I knew he thought he could beat me again, but I wasn't going to let him do it!" What changed? His belief. The ability, the talent, and the victory were always in him . . . he just didn't believe it the first time.

All of the things I would have told him after the tournament about being a champion and believing in himself and losing in his mind before the fight even started, he learned on his own in a single match by switching his focus off of the size of the opponent and onto the size of the champion within himself.

I wonder how often this same scenario plays out in our own lives as we look at the size of our obstacles, the strongholds in our lives that have beaten us in previous rounds, the fear of the loss, and the concern for the pain that happened the last time. In those moments our focus is diverted from the truth that He who is in us is greater than that which has been sent to derail our destiny and steal our gold in the final round!

Pleasing Is Agreeing

The Bible says that without faith (belief) it is impossible to please God and that a person who does not believe should not expect that he will receive anything that God has for him (Hebrews 11:6; James 1:7).

For years I read these verses and thought to myself that if I didn't fully believe, or if I had some doubt in my heart instead of having 100 percent faith, then I was not making God happy, which in my mind meant that I was disappointing Him. But I recently heard a teaching that the word *please* in Hebrews 11:6 implies "to fully agree with," and not necessarily simply "to make happy." That's very different.

The verse could read, "And without faith it's impossible to fully agree with God." And the opposite response to fully agreeing with God is agreeing with the lie of the Devil.

What could be the fallout of not agreeing with God? Well, it could mean that you won't see yourself as He sees you. You will respond according to what *you believe*. You will step on the mat already defeated in your mind, and you will not receive anything that God has for you. Not because He doesn't have better for you, not because it's not yours for the taking, but because your agreement and belief system are focused on a lie that is completely contrary to the truth found in Him.

Is your focus diverted? Is your faith misdirected? God wants to see you win. He has provided the victory for you.

God is greater than your enemy. He's bigger than your failures. Jesus has overcome all the works of the Devil for you. There is a champion inside of you just waiting for you to fully agree with God and take your gold.

If you can see it, you can be it!

Chapter 5

Grace Is Truth

Have you ever said something about someone that you knew you shouldn't have said and they found out about it? How did you respond the next time you saw them? If you are like most, you tried to avoid them. If you saw them in the hallway at school, you went the long way around them or pretended not to see them. If they were in your class, you avoided eye contact so you could escape the intense discomfort you were feeling in that moment. Why? Because you screwed up *and you knew it*! They had a right to be ticked, and if you were in their shoes, you would have been too!

This is a perfect example of what I call *sin consciousness*, and this is the dance that many do with God and church on a weekly basis. We mess up, we know it, and we know that God knows it! At that point we begin to process our relationship and proximity to God based upon what we have been told about Him, how we would feel if we were in God's shoes, and the often accompanied self-loathing that comes as a result of messing up for the umpteenth time over the same stupid issue.

And what do we do? Just like we would do with the friend in school that we talked badly about, we hide, we distance ourselves, and we don't make eye contact with God; we stay out of church for a few weeks or feel guilty when our parents make us go. We wish we did not have to face God or even think about Him because we know we have done what He wouldn't want us to do. Right? And you know what? You're not special or alone in this because we've all done it. We all occasionally ignore or even rebel against what we know is the right thing to do.

What we believe about God and our sin often dictates how we respond to Him. Based on the previous chapters and learning how we respond when we believe a lie, do you think it's possible that what we believe could influence us to do what Satan would want for us, instead of what God would have for us?

Grace Is a Gift

The Bible says that it is by the grace of God (His immense love and favor and desire for greatness toward us in our lives) that we have been saved, through a belief (faith) in Him and His loving grace toward us, and not anything that we have done ourselves, so that ultimately no one can take credit for it by being good enough (Ephesians 2:8–9). The Bible also says that all have sinned and fall short of perfection, and yet it was while *we were in sin* that Christ died for us (Romans 3:23; 5:8).

Forgiveness and salvation through grace are gifts from God because He loves us. If these could be earned or lost by what we did, they would not be a gift. If I gave you a car and then demanded payment for the car, or if I had strings of obligation attached to it, then it wouldn't really be a gift, would it? Yet this is how we often process God and grace. We say we are thankful for the gift of God's grace and that we couldn't possibly earn it. But then we connect strings to it and try to make forgiveness and salvation about us and whether we are worthy to be in God's presence and talk with Him.

In moments like this, our sin consciousness makes our relationship with God about us and the poor choices we have made instead of about Christ and the gift of grace through love.

It's no wonder that we flip-flop in our relationship with God. Through sin consciousness, we are constantly taking a gift that was all about Him and His love for us and making it about our inability to pay for it. Yet that was the entire point of the gift . . . we couldn't pay for it, so Jesus did.

Imagine if someone bought you a car but you chose to continue to walk to work and school every day instead of using that car. Then a couple times a week you went to the person who gave it to you and tried to offer a dollar or two as payment while refusing to drive it until it was completely paid off. What kind of sense does that make for you to not enjoy the gift you have been given because you felt the need to pay for it first?

Yet this is what so many do when it comes to the gift of God and grace. They say, "Thank You, Jesus, for forgiving my sins" and then try to pay Him back or refuse to accept it because they feel like they don't deserve it.

When your sin consciousness becomes your focus, you accept a lie that says you are made clean and acceptable before God based on what you do instead of what Jesus has done for you. From this perspective you can never measure up and God doesn't even intend for you to try to. That's a hopeless place to be and not at all what God wants for you.

Nothing Means Nothing

God loves you, and even in the midst of committing your worst sins, He loves you the same. The Bible says nothing can separate you from God's love (Romans 8:39). This word *nothing* in the original text when properly interpreted means "nothing"!

Embracing this fact of God's unconditional love is absolutely liberating. The Bible says, "You shall know the truth and the truth shall make you free" (John 8:32).

For God was in Christ, restoring the world to himself, no longer counting men's sins against them but blotting them out. This is the wonderful message he has given us to tell others.
(2 Corinthians 5:19 TLB)

Grace is the truth that God has provided for you. He loves you because you are His child. Your sin is not special, and you are not the exception to His love. When the Bible says that the truth shall make you free, it's talking about His loving grace toward you that liberates you from the bondage associated with sin consciousness. Your sins are covered and He loves you!

Then he adds:

*"Their sins and lawless acts
I will remember no more."
And where these have been forgiven, sacrifice for sin is no longer
necessary.*
(Hebrews 10:17–18)

*And I will forgive their wickedness,
and I will never again remember their sins.*
(Hebrews 8:12 NLT)

Don't run from God. That's what the Devil would like for you to do, creating distance between you and the One who makes you perfect. Instead, run to God and allow His grace and love to melt away the sin in your life.

You are forgiven, you are loved, and you are clean in God's eyes. Not because of what you have done, but because of what Christ did for you!

Chapter 6

Jesus Is the Truth

Jesus said in the Bible, "I am the way and the truth and the life" (John 14:6). In other words, we find our way to a relationship with God, the truth, and the ability to live as God intended for us through (and because of) Christ.

In the previous chapter I stated, "Grace is truth." Jesus said that if we have seen Him, we have seen the Father, and that He did nothing that He hadn't seen or heard the Father do (John 14:7–9; John 5:19; 12:49). When we study the Gospels in the Bible (Matthew, Mark, Luke, and John), we see the life of Christ made clear from the written perspective of four of His disciples. The word *gospel* means "good news." Jesus came to restore our relationship with God and to show us the good news of how great the love of God actually is toward us.

As we study the life of Christ, we see that He exampled grace everywhere He went.

Did Jesus ever condemn anyone? *No.*

Did He ever make someone sick to teach them a lesson or draw them closer to God? *No.*

When the woman was caught in the act of adultery (a sin punishable by death at that time), did He judge her? *No. He showed her love and extended grace to her.*

When the prostitute took perfume valued at a year's worth of wages that she made sinning with untold multiples of men and poured it on Jesus' feet, did He correct her, condemn her, or ostracize her? *No. He accepted her in love.*

When the thief on the cross asked Him to remember him in heaven, did He belittle or reject him? *No. He promised the man he would be with Him in heaven.*

Jesus didn't make people feel bad about themselves. He didn't look for ways to hurt them in order to teach them. He didn't shame them or belittle them to show them He was the boss so they would come to a place of repentance. He didn't make anyone feel condemned because of their mistakes or sins. He didn't ever curse or pass severe judgment on anyone because they didn't measure up. Jesus loved those He came in contact with! And remember, Jesus said, "Anyone who has seen me has seen the Father" (John 14:9). In other words, He said, "Watch Me, and what you see in Me is a perfect representation of who God really is, despite what you've been taught to believe." As a matter of fact, the only ones we see Jesus really getting angry with are the ones who misrepresented or twisted the love of His Father and distorted who He really was and what His Word said!

Just because you may have been told that God is a lightning bolt–wielding tyrant sitting on the edge of eternity, just waiting for you to screw up so He can teach you a good lesson and show you that He's God and you're not, doesn't mean that's who He is! Is it possible that people have created an image of God based on who they would be if they were God, or how they think God should feel about us when we sin? Maybe they attempt to manipulate people with fear and judgment so others will do what they tell them to do to justify their own ego-driven power trip. But that's not how God works.

In Jesus' day, many of the religious leaders took an ungodly approach to teaching about who God is, and today this lying "religious spirit" still seeks to paint an image of God and His grace in such a way that it seems truly unattainable. I believe this is because if God becomes unreachable and grace becomes unattainable in your mind, then your pursuit and your experience will be limited by your beliefs. It's a form of control.

But Jesus!

Jesus came so that we could know the truth about God, so we could see the perfect example of who God really is and how

Jesus Is the Truth

God really feels about us. He did so knowing that truth of God's love and grace toward us would make us free (John 8:32).

There are so many wrong religious opinions accepted about who God is, how He feels about sin, how He feels about us, and whether we are who God says we are based upon what we did yesterday. My only response is this: Jesus Christ is the example of perfect truth as it pertains to how we view God. If Jesus said that God loves us and is not holding our sin against us, then *that is the truth of who God is*!

You should question anything that someone says is a characteristic of God that does not line up perfectly with the exampled life of Christ. (In order to do this, however, you need to know about the life of Christ. Read the gospels so you can discern the truth from any distortions.) And I would say that if you are receiving advice from someone that does not line up with Jesus' words and actions, toss it out.

The truth of what Jesus said about His Father trumps anything that anyone else has to say. You are loved, forgiven, and righteous because God says you are—not because you earned it and not because you deserve it. God loves you because He said He does. This is the truth because He said it is. The opinions of the rest are just worthless words spoken with a lot of hot air.

Chapter 7

Jesus Restored What Sin Destroyed

Genesis teaches us that God created man in His image and likeness to have relationship with Him. He gave man authority on the earth with the intent of teaching him how to use that authority to rule with the wisdom of God and establish the kingdom of God (God's way of doing things) on the earth.

Sin came between man and God and kept us from being able to learn directly from God by personally communicating with Him as He intended. As a result, knowing Him completely became impossible.

This separation came at a great cost to man, and for thousands of years, he was limited to hearing the voice of God through the imperfect, sin-tainted vessels of chosen leaders and prophets who didn't always represent Him well. All of them interpreted God and His words through the lenses of imperfection. Some of these messengers became arrogant; other's fell into depravity. All of them had their own faults. All of them were jaded and limited by their experiences and ability to interpret God's intent with full clarity.

Their full understanding of who God is was limited by their humanity. Even language created a barrier for the message of God—much like today.

Think about it. Have you ever felt something very strongly, but when you tried to express it, words were inadequate? If God revealed something perfectly to them, the moment it was placed in language it became tainted by the imperfection and limitation of that language.

Still, God inspired (which means "breathed upon") their words and their leadership. And in His perfection, He was able to work within the limitations of man's imperfection to continue to move humanity forward in their journey toward knowing Him. Ultimately His plan was that they could experience the perfection that would be found in His Son, who was untainted by sin and could perfectly convey the heart of the Father in a new and perfect covenant.

That Which Was Lost

According to Luke 19:10, in His perfect love for us, God sent Jesus to restore "that which was lost" (NASB). The *that* referred to in Luke 19:10 is everything that was lost because of sin. God gave man authority on the earth and always intended to have a personal and intimate relationship with him. He always intended to personally teach mankind and use us to establish His will and kingdom here on earth.

Jesus restored our relationship, our intimacy, our authority, and our ability to personally connect with and communicate with the God of the cosmos, the God who created an entire universe. (Fun fact: science has proven the universe has more stars in it than grains of sand in every beach and desert on earth. Although the numbers vary greatly depending upon who does the calculation, it's speculated that there are 7.5 x 10 to the 18th power grains of sand, or somewhere around seven quintillion five hundred quadrillion grains.[1] Yet there is somewhere between 10 sextillion and a septillion stars in our universe!)

The God who created *that* created *you* to have an intimate and intentional relationship with Him. He wants to be our God and for us to be His people and for us to seek first His kingdom and bring it with victory and authority to every place on earth.

Quite honestly, I'm blown away by this thought, yet I'm ecstatic by the proposition. The God of the universe knows me, loves me, wants me, supports me, provides for me, fights for me, protects me, surrounds me, instructs me, encourages me, commissions me, empowers me, and backs me. Truly believing in

---

[1] Visit www.npr.org for more fascinating science facts.

and fully agreeing with the limitless love, grace, power, authority, and relationship with *that* God has a way of revolutionizing behaviors, transforming experiences, and liberating existences.

Right Believing Leads to Right Living

Right believing leads to right living. Knowing, truly knowing, this truth will set you free. When who God is and how He feels about you become more real to you than what you feel you are not, there's not a devil in hell or a battle before you that has the power to intimidate you or hold you back!

God, because of His overwhelming love for us, paid the price that we couldn't pay to empower us to be who we otherwise could never be. Jesus Christ was the example of everything we were created to be before sin and the limitations that came along with it kept us from our destiny! Jesus showed us what it looks like when we are in relationship with God and being led by Him, not bound by the influence of our enemy, the Devil.

Is it possible that what we believe has influenced our current reality? The Bible says that God's people die for a lack of knowledge (Hosea 4:6). Could it be that you have not really understood who God is and how He *truly* feels about you? If so, this lack of knowledge has subsequently kept you from becoming the powerful kingdom-establishing, sin-destroying, victorious representative of God that you were created to be. Walking in the power He has created you to walk in over sin has *nothing* to do with your age or the amount of time you have been a Christian. In Bible days, people entered into a relationship with God one day and the next day they were changing their world because they understood and believed that they could.

What if I told you there is more than what you have experienced?

What if I told you that you don't have to be bound by sin?

What if I told you that you are the idea of a loving God?

What if I told you that God always intended for you to be more than you have become?

What if I told you He wanted it for you more than you want it for yourself?

Jesus Restored What Sin Destroyed

I'm telling you these things now because *there is more*. You don't have to be bound. He has always intended for you to be more. He wants it for you more than you want it for yourself, and the sooner you can grasp this truth in life, the better off you will be!

I wish someone had enough insight to teach me this stuff when I was a young adult. I didn't learn much of what is in this book regarding the freedom, power, and potential that I had in Christ until I was well into my thirties. So you are getting a jump start on experiencing the limitless freedom that God has for you that I didn't have.

God has an amazing plan for your life, and I'm telling you, it's an awesome one!

> *Before I formed you in the womb I knew you*
> *[and approved of you as My chosen instrument],*
> *And before you were born I consecrated you*
> *[to Myself as My own].*
> (Jeremiah 1:5 AMP)

In the next section, we will discuss who you really are from God's perspective. Get ready, your perceptions are about to be challenged and your life is about to change!

Part II

Who Am I?

For part II of this book we will build upon the understanding initially established in part I by presenting a clear case regarding *who we are* from God's perspective.

There are conflicting voices competing for our attention and attempting to influence our resolve. But why? Is it possible that our enemy, the Devil, has attacked our minds regarding how we see ourselves? If we embrace the truth about who we really are, then his ability to influence us and use us for his purposes becomes impacted.

The truth of who we are may be very different from who we believe we are. But our belief systems absolutely influence our outcomes. In part II, we are going to confront some of the lies that we have embraced and learn why it's important that we see ourselves through proper lenses in order to experience the Freedom Revolution that God has provided for us.

Chapter 8

How You See Yourself Matters

Few things influence our outcomes as much as how we see ourselves. Henry Ford said, "If you think you can or you think you can't you are right!" In previous chapters we have talked about who God is, and in the next few we are going to be addressing who we are.

As a youth pastor for my first decade of ministry, and as a pastor who has traveled the world speaking in public schools and churches since then, I've encountered so many people (including myself) who have gone through difficult times. Everywhere I go, I encounter people who have had the rug yanked out from underneath them, experienced betrayal from friends and loved ones, been abused, felt forgotten by everyone (sometimes even God) and found themselves questioning, "Why am I here? What is my purpose? Who am I really?"

I have asked these same questions, not just in my teen years, but as an adult during different seasons in my life both as a pastor and a law enforcement officer. There was actually a time when I was so disillusioned with my life that I told my wife I was going to give up being a pastor all together and focus completely on being a cop. Thankfully, I had a wife who reminded me who I was and what God had called me to when circumstances made it difficult for me to remember on my own.

Isn't it interesting how feelings of worthlessness can influence how you process life and affect your behaviors? Like you, I went through times in my life when I wasn't sure how God felt about me. I wasn't happy with my life experience. I was very confused by some of the events that happened to me that I didn't feel were fair, and I didn't know how to get past them.

Years ago I was hired as a youth pastor by a pastor who made a lot of promises to me regarding the pay I would receive, the exposure he would help me experience, and the opportunities he would provide if I agreed to work with him. I moved several states away from my family to be a part of his church, but after a few years of working with him, none of the promises were fulfilled—not one of them. Then out of nowhere, he packed up and left without even telling me he was leaving. In that season I felt like much of what I had invested was simply wasted time and energy, and I felt very used. I was mad at him, and I was a bit irritated with God because I was confident that He told me to move to Tennessee to be a part of this ministry. (In hindsight I can say that there were things that God was working in to turn around for my good in spite of the pastor, but I didn't have the insight then that I do now.)

I found myself feeling very discouraged and alone. During that time the enemy threw a party in my mind and attempted to convince me that church, my relationship with God, and my contribution to His kingdom were pointless.

In that season I wrote this poem expressing my frustration and internal struggle with anger, judgment, and sin. Maybe you've been there yourself. Maybe you will be able to identify.

Who Am I, Really?

There's conflict inside of me
With so much I want to be
And so much I want to see
But so much that cannot be
There's two sides that make me, me
And both sides won't let me be
At war most constantly
Tearing apart internally
How am I to find victory
When for trees the forest cannot be seen
A general with no army to lead

How You See You Matters

> A vocalist with no song to sing
> A visionary with only shattered dreams
> A musician with only broken strings
> Trying to grasp what's just out of reach
> Wanting to understand what no one can teach
> Striving to share with no words to speak
> And the answer to one question I seek . . .
> . . . after all, who am I, really?

Within every man, woman, and child lies an innate desire to matter and have purpose. Yet in my own life I couldn't see the purpose. I felt different from others and in many ways very alone.

As I said earlier, I have also experienced these kinds of feelings as a pastor and as a cop. I went into law enforcement to help compensate for my lack of income as a youth pastor, so I was a pastor, a detective sergeant, and a SWAT team member all at the same time.

My Story

On the last day of my career as a cop, I arrested a couple of young men (seventeen and eighteen years old) who had snuck out of a rehabilitation home the night before and stolen some things from several of the neighborhood cars and garages in the surrounding area. They were honest with me and agreed to help me get the stolen property back to the proper people, and I in turn agreed to speak with the judge to request leniency in their punishment. However, while we were out returning the stolen property, they conspired to kill me.

Long story short, they attacked me, striking me in the face with a trailer hitch. Then I was thrown from my vehicle at around forty-five miles per hour. My nose was shattered, I lost some teeth, my lip was split nearly in two, and when my head hit the asphalt from being flung out of my car, both of my inner ears busted. I spent the next year in physical therapy, on emotion- and anxiety-suppressing drugs for PTSD, and then at the end of that year, because of the inner-ear injuries and the concern the doctors still had with them, I was let go from my job with no pension or compensation.

Then, in 2008, the US economy tanked, and I couldn't get a job. It was a brutal season for a man who had worked as close to full-time as I could since I was fourteen years old. I couldn't provide for my family, my wife was working ten to twelve hours a day to support us, I had a newborn son I really had no idea how to take care of, I was depressed, I felt alone, and in many ways, I felt abandoned. I, the former extreme extrovert, became a recluse and all but hid from people. I lost my laughter. I lost my hope. I saw myself as a failure. And it influenced everything else in my life.

God Is Still Faithful
Mark Twain said, "The two most important days in your life are the day you are born and the day you find out why." A few years into my recovery, I quietly said to God, "Don't You think I've been in this season a long time?" I didn't expect an answer, but the one I got was even more unexpected. As clear as day came the immediate response, "Aaron, you had a lot to unlearn."

It's amazing how much that little moment of clarity gave me hope. The revelation that God was using that which the Devil intended for my destruction to better me, teach me, and advance me gave me hope. It was from that moment forward that I began to pursue a clearer understanding of who God really is, how He feels about me, and who I am as His son.

For You formed my innermost parts;
You knit me [together] in my mother's womb.
I will give thanks and praise to You, for I am fearfully and
wonderfully made;
Wonderful are Your works,
And my soul knows it very well.
(Psalm 139:13–14 AMP)

I began to see how my having a very different personality and wiring was on purpose, and it allowed me to bring something to the table that wouldn't be there if I didn't offer it. I began to see myself and my value through God's eyes. I realized I am worthy, I am equipped, and I am commissioned! I realized that there are no scar-less warriors, and that leaders worth following often walk with a limp. My experiences and battle scars hadn't disqualified me from leadership; they put me in the perfect position for more effective leadership.

These realizations inspired in me a new purpose to go on and pursue the dreams I had lost in the previous season. Although the revelation came immediately, learning how to accept it and implement it took a long time.

> *For God's gifts and his call can never be withdrawn; he will never go back on his promises.*
> (Romans 11:29 TLB)

Still, He who began a good work in me was faithful to bring it to a place of completion. He wasn't content to allow tragedy to be the last word in my life, and instead used the tragedy to position me for triumph!

In many ways, I'm still learning daily who I was created to be as God builds off of the progress of yesterday in pursuit of tomorrow's dreams and promises. I came to understand that God can take that which was intended to take me out and use it as a catalyst for my next level of advancement. And He can do that for you as well.

The two best days are the day you were born and the day you find out why. Are you ready to find out why?

Chapter 9

As a Man Thinks . . .

The Bible says in Proverbs 23:7, "As [a man] thinks in his heart, so is he" (NKJV). This is a pretty powerful statement that I have seen played out so many times and in multitudes of ways. Whether a multimillionaire or the poorest of the poor, through winning and losing, learning to succeed or remaining in a rut, so many times how a person views their situation influences how they pursue their outcomes.

I believe that this is also one of the most significant aspects when remaining bound by sin and never really reaching a place of true freedom. The Bible says, "If the Son sets you free, you will be free indeed" (John 8:36). Yet I can say with all assurance that, even as a pastor, for a majority of my life I felt like I'd take one step forward and get knocked back two steps.

I felt like I was part of the crowd in the stands still cheering, "We're gonna win!" with all the rest of the cheerleaders my team was losing 97 to nothing and there were only a few minutes left in the game. Sure, it felt good to say what everyone wanted to believe, but I really didn't believe I was going to win (unless winning was defined as being able to walk away instead of crawling after another loss).

Growing up, I was told frequently that I was a sinner saved by grace. It was delivered in such a way that I kind of understood that God covered the sin, but I processed it like a label that defined me. Even though I knew God loved me, I still saw myself branded with the "Sinner" label.

As a Man Thinks...

Imagine if you had a parent or teacher who told you every Sunday, "You're stupid and you will always be stupid, but because of who your dad is, he'll still help you make it in life." That's how I understood sin and grace. In my mind, because of this definition of being a sinner, even though I would still go to heaven because of the grace of God, I was always going to be *a sinner*, which to me meant that I was always going to be defined by sin and forever bound by it. As a result, I associated my worth with feeling as though I was *tolerated* but not *cherished*. This label left me feeling tarnished and hopeless to overcome sin.

Don't get me wrong—I was thankful for a daddy who was going to help me make it anyway. But in my mind I was still the stupid one and believed that even my heavenly Father thought so. For me, the battle was lost before it began. Why would I aspire to be more if I didn't believe I could be?

Renewing Your Mind

About six years ago I began comparing what the Bible said about the grace and love of God with what I had been taught about myself and about God throughout the years, and I discovered something very interesting. Not everything I had been taught as the truth was what the Bible said was the truth!

I began to research the Bible. I looked at the authors of the books of the Bible, who each book was written to, why the writers wrote what they did, whether there was anything that could have been misunderstood between the language in which the books were written and the current interpretations today. And I was astounded by what was revealed.

I discovered was that although it was true that I was a sinner and bound by sin before entering into a relationship with God through Christ, when I entered into that covenant with God, everything changed!

I read in Ephesians 2 that before the power of God came into my life, sin was my master and I was spiritually dead. But a metamorphosis took place and my sinful nature was obliterated when I trusted in Christ.

I read in Colossians 2 that even though I was dead, I was made alive in Christ.

I read in Romans 3, 5, 8, and 10 that when I was in sin Jesus died for me and purchased my freedom.

I read in Galatians 1 that Jesus rescued me from the bondage of sin.

I read in Romans 3 and 2 Corinthians 5 that I am made righteous by Christ.

And the learning went on and on!

Don't copy the behavior and customs of this world, but let God transform you into a new person by changing the way you think. Then you will learn to know God's will for you, which is good and pleasing and perfect.
(Romans 12:2 NLT)

It's amazing to me that according to Romans 12:2, the way I think has the capacity to transform me into a new person, and then I can gain understanding about God's perfect will for my life.

The most liberating and transforming I discovered—once my mind was changed and I saw myself as God sees me—was that my label is not "Sinner saved by grace," which to me meant that I was tolerated by God. On the contrary, I was a sinner before Christ revolutionized my life, but now I've been transformed by the grace of God. My label and existence is now "Righteousness."

I am (just like you are if you accepted Christ), in God's eyes, clean and in right standing with Him. I'm not the stupid kid and the constant screw-up. On the contrary, because I'm His son, I've received a completely transformative miracle. Like a caterpillar to a butterfly, I have been completely redesigned and defined by a new level of beauty and existence.

I'm not bound to walk around in a measly ground-level existence . . . not anymore! I've been given wings of grace and righteousness to fly above what used to be the limitations of a ground-bound existence! That boulder, or fence, or tree, or mountain of sin that used to be insurmountable in my own strength now has become little more than something for me to observe when I fly over it with my new wings.

Did you know that you do not have to be bound by sin and that you can live free from it? You can by coming to the place of understanding who you are and what that entitles you to. First Corinthians 15:34 says to awake to righteousness and sin not.

Experiencing the limitless freedom, power, and potential that God created you for begins when you start to believe at a heart level who He has transformed you into and *awake to the righteousness* of who you really are, giving you the strength to *sin not*. Romans 12:2 states that you are not conformed to this world but transformed by the renewing of your mind. Basically, you prove the will of God for His people when you learn to think differently.

You already *are* more than you probably know and believe. Awake to the righteousness of who you are and what you have in Christ.

Sin no longer defines you.

Chapter 10

I Will Remember Their Sin No More

If your teen experience has been anything like mine was, you have likely been presented with a laundry list of what you have to do or not do if you are to be a good Christian and please God. So many rules, so much sin, so much to feel unworthy about. It has the potential to be overwhelming, doesn't it?

I recently heard a pastor say, "Sin separates us from God." I'm not sure that is always true. For the one who has not entered into covenant with God and been made alive in Christ, I would agree that our sin creates a barrier between where we are and where God desires for us to be. But when Jesus said, "It is finished" on the cross (John 19:30), He covered every single one of our past sins and every sin that we would ever commit.

For those who *are* in Christ, sin no longer separates us because we are no longer sinners. Jesus was the perfect sacrifice, and we no longer have to *earn* our place or offer any additional sacrifice. Remember, the scripture says, "Awake to your righteousness!" (1 Corinthians 15:34). Or in other words, "Open your eyes and see yourself as you are—righteous in the eyes of God."

A failure on our end does not disrupt the terms of our covenant. Man's failure to hold up his end of the covenant with God was the reason that all the covenants in the Old Testament made between God and man were imperfect. In his own power and bound by sin, man could not be good enough or faithful enough to keep the terms. So God took man and sin out of the scenario. His perfect and sinless Son became the final sacrifice, and He established a covenant in perfection that was—and will forever be—unblemished by the influence of sin.

Grace Is Truth

The book of Hebrews describes in great detail the amazing depth of this new covenant established in Christ between God and man. And in Hebrews 10:17, God says, "Their sins and lawless acts I will remember no more." I love the words *I will* in this verse. Have you ever considered their meaning? *I will* means "I submit my will to." In other words, God is saying in Hebrews 10, "Because of the sacrifice of My Son and the new perfect covenant that I have established with man, I submit My will to remember their sin no more," or "Although I used to, it is no longer My will to remember their sin or hold them accountable for it."

That is so powerful! Yes, we were once dead and lost in our sin, but since we have been made alive in Christ, God has chosen to no longer remember our sin or hold it against us.

In the Old Testament (old covenant), the Law (the Ten Commandments and 613 rules derived from them) showed what would be necessary to perfectly please God, and quite honestly, it was impossible. Ultimately, it just revealed how ridiculously inadequate we are when it's up to us to make ourselves clean in God's sight.

Under the new covenant, God said, "It is now time to cover sin once and for all, restore man to the place of authority on the earth that I created him to have, reconcile the relationship that he was originally created to have with Me, and give him a level playing field where sin is not an absolute controlling factor. And to really take the power from sin, I'm not going to hold sin against him or allow it to create a wedge once he is in covenant with Me."

Astounding, isn't it?

In John 1:17, the Bible says that the law came through Moses but grace and truth came through Jesus. When looking at the original text, grace and truth are presented in such a way that the construction of the sentence indicates they are synonymous. In other words, the grace *is* truth and the truth *is* grace!

Several years ago my friend Tony Sutherland wrote a book titled *Grace Works* and asked me to review it before publishing. As a pastor, I thought I understood the subject of grace and intended to offer some constructive criticism on how he could make what he wrote better. Little did I know, my life and theology were about to change as I read about grace and the love God had for me in a way that I had never been taught or even considered. Every objection I came up with as I read was refuted by scriptures that presented the case for grace in a way that, in the end, I could not dispute. That meant, even as a pastor, *I had been wrong about how God felt about me my whole life.*

When I came to the realization of how God really felt about me, that my sin was covered in a way that God didn't even see it and that His grace was a gift I not only did not have to earn but couldn't earn, at that moment, after more than thirty years of struggling and losing the fight against sin, sin lost its power to control me.

I came to actually know and understand the truth of the grace of God. It was in my discovery of the truth about who God is, who I am, how He feels about me, what He did for me, and how sin no longer condemned me that I experienced the revolution of freedom!

For you shall know the truth and the truth shall make you free! Grace is the truth, and the truth is grace.

Does that mean I never sinned again? Nope! The difference is that guilt and feelings of failure used to control how I approached God. It felt like I had slimy oil around me because of sin consciousness. Now those feels just roll off me like water off of a duck's back because I know God loves me and is for me, in spite of my mistakes.

I'm convinced that Christians who genuinely believe that God loves them and understand the true depth of love and grace of God toward them are not controlled by sin. This knowledge does not (as many assume) give us a freedom to sin, but actually empowers us *not to sin.*

> *God saved you by his grace when you believed. And you can't take credit for this; it is a gift from God. Salvation is not a reward for the good things we have done, so none of us can boast about it. For we are God's masterpiece.*

I Will Remember Their Sin No More

He has created us anew in Christ Jesus, so we can do the good things he planned for us long ago.
(Ephesians 2:8–10 NLT)

When we awaken to righteousness through the grace of God, we actually have the power not to sin, like the scripture says. Something spiritual clicks in the mind, and what we believe empowers us to be who God intended for us to be all along.

When our relationship with God and His love toward us becomes about us keeping the rules, it's no longer about the good news, but rather about somehow earning what He says He gave us as a gift. Thank God that because of His grace, we have been given the ability to do and be who He always intended for us to be—free from sin and empowered by Him!

Chapter 11

No Condemnation

I recently saw a video of a bulldog that had eaten a hole in the arm of the couch while the owner was away. The dog would not move away from the hole in the couch and covered it with his body. The owner would tell the dog to move and show him what he had done, but the dog, with the most shame-filled look on his face, refused to move and continued to try to block and hide his sin from his master.

I found it so funny yet similar to how we often act when we mess up. Riddled by guilt, we somehow hope that by pretending we didn't sin or hiding our sin, maybe the Master won't notice.

In this video, the master recorded the dog's action with a video camera, and although the dog was obviously very emotionally involved in the scenario, the owner behind the camera simply and unemotionally asked the dog over and over again to show him what he was hiding. He really wasn't upset by the dog making a dog kind of a mistake; he just wanted the dog to be honest about it.

If we confess our sins, he is faithful and just and will forgive us our sins and purify us from all unrighteousness.
(1 John 1:9)

The moment you choose to sin, God knows about it. Like the bulldog in the video, you aren't hiding it from God; you are just stewing in the condemnation of something God is asking you to own up to instead of pretending that you are fooling Him by attempting to hide it. When you confess your sin, God isn't surprised or taken aback by your confession. When the Bible tells us to confess our sin to God, it isn't to inform God of what He already knows; it's just the moment when you release it from the power to control you anymore through condemnation.

> *There is therefore now no condemnation to them which are in Christ Jesus.*
> (Romans 8:1 KJV)

Although the Bible says that we as believers do not suffer condemnation from God, I've heard many church leaders teach quite a contradictory gospel (at least in my experience).

So what is condemnation? Here's the definition, according to Google:

con·dem·na·tion
kändəm ˈnāSH(ə)n/
noun
1. The expression of very strong disapproval; censure.
"there was strong international condemnation of the attack"
synonyms:
censure, criticism, *strictures*, denunciation, vilification
2. The action of condemning someone to a punishment; sentencing.

When I looked up the definition of *condemnation*, I thought about how many times in my life I have believed that I would experience some kind of condemnation from God, even when His Word says that I do not.

God doesn't have any problem separating us and our sin from the finished work of Christ on the cross, but for whatever reason, *we* really do, don't we? It's just difficult to accept that God loves us and doesn't hold sin against His children. But it's essential for our progress that we come to a place of understanding and agreeing with God on this issue if we are to experience the limitless freedom that Christ purchased for us!

For God so loved the world that he gave his one and only Son, that whoever believes in him shall not perish but have eternal life. For God did not send his Son into the world to condemn the world, but to save the world through him.
(John 3:16–17)

Is It a Gift or Not?

As we discussed in the previous chapter, what Christ purchased for us was a gift from God according to Ephesians 2:8, not something to bring further guilt, condemnation, or separation. God is not trying to keep anyone out, alienate anyone, or condemn anyone. Completely to the contrary, through the gift of His grace, He has provided a way for none to be excluded by their faults or shortcomings!

How weird would it be to bring a gift to a birthday party, hand the birthday boy your beautifully wrapped gift, then reach in your pocket, pull out the receipt, give it to him, and say, "You can pay me later." Yet this is what our actions toward God reveal about how we view Him as a gift giver when we act as though His gift comes with strings attached.

God says that grace is a gift we cannot pay for, so why do we insist on trying to pay for it and earn it? Doing so is insulting to the giver of the gift when we act like we believe He demands payment for what He gave freely from His love.

Remember, when the Bible says in Romans 8:39 that nothing can separate us from the love of God, the word *nothing* in this scripture means "nothing." You can't earn God's love, and your sin can't separate you from Him either! His grace isn't for sale to those who keep the rules better than you do. You are not excluded from His love because of what you did yesterday, last week, or last year. God loves you and accepts you and forgives you as much as any other person.

The love and grace of God is good news that you can be excited about. Regardless of what you thought you knew, you are accepted, not condemned.

I have a dear pastor friend who many years ago was an international drug dealer. He got busted, and based on the charges brought against him, he was likely going to go to prison for a long

No Condemnation

time. In a miracle occurrence (that as a former law enforcement officer I still don't fully understand), the charges against him were dropped and his record was wiped clean. It's crazy! By all rights, he should be in prison today, but somehow grace was extended beyond his ability to deserve or earn it. The grace extended toward him was actually instrumental in his life being transformed. Now he pastors and helps others.

He doesn't sell drugs anymore because in the face of punishment, the grace given to him changed how he thinks about that lifestyle. He appreciates the freedom that grace has provided for him. He was awakened by grace to righteousness, and as a result, that sinful lifestyle doesn't have power over him today.

In light of awakening to the grace of God in your life, how might that change how you respond to God and the choices you make for your own life? Choices are influenced by belief systems, which is why awakening to the possibility of more influences your ability to experience more.

When the Bible says, "There is therefore now no condemnation for those who are in Christ Jesus," there's not a whole lot of wiggle room for us to believe anything differently.

*N*o is an absolute . . . which means *no* or *none*.

No means no . . .

You're not condemned. You are righteous in God's eyes.

Chapter 12

Spirit, Soul, and Body

Because most of our information comes through our physical senses, it is very easy to become more aware of *our physical reality* at the cost of *spiritual* awareness. However, God exists and operates in a realm that we have come to understand as *spiritual* (or *the spirit realm*) and created all that we understand as *physical* from that realm. So, although our awareness of the spiritual realm and its influences may be much more limited, I believe it's important to ask, "What's more real—the creation or its Creator?"

Just because we cannot see into the spiritual realm with our physical eyes does not make it any less real. In truth, it could very well be that the spirit realm is *more* physical than our realm (or even a much more complex extension of it); we just can't physically see it. I realize that seems difficult to process based on what we have been taught about heaven and God and Spirit, but just track with me here for a moment.

In quantum physics, scientists have calculated that there are at least eleven dimensions to our current understanding of physical reality, even though humanly we are only cognizant of four (length, width, height, and time, otherwise known as the space-time continuum). Some of you high school students may have learned about the space-time continuum in your science classes.

Scientists have created tests involving particle collision in particle accelerators (a machine that accelerates some of the smallest particles of matter to nearly light speeds and then crashes them into each other to observe the effects) and discovered that fragments of the collided particles have vanished from sight and then reappeared in other places. Imagine Star Trek–style teleportation, but on a much smaller scale.

So where did the particles go? It's theorized that they are disappearing into these "other unobservable dimensions" and then reappearing in our observable dimensions. In theory, it would not be far-fetched to propose that God actually more perfectly exists in these additional (technically physical) dimensions although we are limited in our perception of them.

Spirit or Soul?

Each of us has been created in the image of God and has an eternal *spirit*. That spirit resides within our physical bodies, which is primarily controlled by our *souls* (consisting of our mind, will, and emotions which communicates between our physical body and our spirit "man" via the supercomputer that God has given every person on earth, also known as our brain). I heard neuroscientist Dr. Caroline Leaf describe it this way (and I am paraphrasing in layman's terms): If the brain is the physical computer, the soul is the software.[2]

People often confuse the terms *spirit* and *soul*, assuming them to be the same . . . but they are not. Your soul consists of your mind, your will, and your emotions. Your soul communicates to your physical body but also interprets what your spirit discerns when God is communicating with you. Your soul is the link that God created to bridge a dimensional gap between the understood physicality and the spirit realm (whatever the spirit realm will be defined as or understood to be in the future). Because our soul has the potential to discern and interpret both physical and spiritual information, many times we find it torn and warring between what our physical man and our spiritual man desires.

When we become Christians and enter into a relationship with God, it is our spirit that experiences a metamorphosis and is made alive and radically transformed, not our bodies. And

---

[2] For a more in-depth study on the fascinating subject of spirit, soul, and body, check out http://drleaf.com/broadcast/.

sometimes our mind needs to be reprogrammed to line up with God's way of doing things.

Just because access to the truth is available does not mean that we will pursue the truth, let alone believe it. And we have already discussed how what we *believe* influences our actions. Because we have spent a lifetime interpreting information primarily through our physical senses, there is often a struggle in learning to process spiritual things beyond what our senses can understand. And sometimes the conflicting information between what physical senses interpret as truth what our spirit tells us is the truth leaves our soul (mind, will, and emotions) with the responsibility of deciding *which truth* we will believe.

A very plain example of this is that although I know that I am saved and loved by God and that His grace perfectly covers all of my sins, sometimes I *feel* like I'm not saved, and it doesn't always take an earth-shattering event to cause that feeling. I could be walking through my dark bedroom at 3:00 a.m., stub my pinky toe on the corner of the bed, and completely lose any resemblance of a relationship with God. In that moment, the pastor in me vanishes, and the ungodly mix of pain and rage may release a verbal outburst of unholiness that leaves me feeling less than saved. If you asked me in that moment how saved I feel, you might get an earful that would make you doubt my salvation.

I believe God's Word and my spirit man bears witness to the truth that I am made alive in Christ, yet sometimes my emotions and logic do not line up with what my spirit knows to be true. My mind and will are left with the decision to extend belief and faith between what my emotions feel and what my spirit knows.

Those who make a habit of relying primarily upon their emotions to navigate life (especially their spiritual life) will have an experience that is as flighty and fickle as their emotions. And anyone who has ever been in a relationship with another human being knows that emotions can change as quickly as the weather. This is why it is essential to determine what is the truth and then decide that we will stand upon that truth no matter what our emotions try to say.

Spirit, Soul, and Body

When your mind, will, and emotions say, *Man, I've really screwed up this time*, or *I think I've really stepped outside the realm of God's ability to love me*, or *I'm simply not worthy to experience what God's Word says is mine*, your determination to stand upon the truth of God's Word trumps the reality of your current emotional state or temporary physical perception of truth. In those situations, say, *No! God says I am His. I am loved, accepted, and covered.*

In that moment, we determine what the truth is, we extend faith toward that truth, and we stand upon that truth in spite of the circumstances! "Then you will know the truth, and the truth will set you free" (John 8:32).

Chapter 13

God's Provision and the Wages of Sin

Do you know anyone who is really experiencing the complete fullness of what God's Word said was possible and Jesus exampled? Probably not.

The Bible says that you are the righteousness of God (in complete right standing with God) in Christ Jesus (Romans 3:22), that you are a joint heir with Christ (all that was available to and in Christ is available to you) (Romans 8:17), that you were created in the image of God (Genesis 1:27), that you are more than a conqueror (Romans 8:31–39), that nothing shall separate you from the love of God (Romans 8:35), that God is not holding your sin against you (2 Corinthians 5:19; Hebrews 8:12), and that Jesus came to give you life to the full (John 10:10). Yet it also says that the wages of sin is death (Romans 6:23). So what are we to believe?

Anyone who has been a Christian more than a week has likely asked some hard questions like this one. And it's okay to ask questions. God can handle it! He's not offended by your lack of understanding. Nor is He threatened by one of His children asking Him to help them understand what doesn't make sense to them. There was even a time in the Bible when Jesus asked a man if he believed and his honest answer was, "I do believe; help me overcome my unbelief" (Mark 9:24). It's okay to be straight with God. He meets you where you are, and if you are looking for answers, He will help you find what you are looking for.

How the Garden of Eden Impacted Our Reality

God's Provision and the Wages of Sin

I think the beginning of finding answers to some of these hard questions starts with defining what was lost in the Garden of Eden when man sinned, as well as understanding what Christ restored in the new covenant.

When God created man, He gave him complete authority on earth, and He intended to personally teach him how to perfectly rule by implementing God's principles on the earth. Before man sinned in the Garden of Eden, he walked with God, had an intimate and personal relationship with Him, and was able to directly approach God for instruction, wisdom, and guidance. There was nothing separating Adam and Eve from God, and they were completely righteous (in right standing with God).

When Adam sinned, an opposing kingdom of sin was introduced that was in direct opposition to God's kingdom and His way of doing things. God's kingdom brought life and peace, but the kingdom of sin brought death and destruction.

In addition to the kingdom of sin being established on the earth, sin also created a barrier and separation between man and God. Adam and Eve chose to be their own king when they disregarded God's way of learning directly from Him. They decided they didn't fully trust Him when they believed the lies the Devil told them and assumed that God was hiding something from them, so they tried to do things their own way.

We read in a previous chapter that without faith (belief) it is impossible to please and come into full agreement with God. And Adam in the garden (through his blatant disobedience) showed God that he didn't fully have faith and trust in Him.

When you believe the lie, you empower the liar. And Satan, by deceiving man into sin, was given authority on earth. The Bible says in Romans 6:23 that the wages (cost) of sin is death. When sin entered the earth and separated us from God, the wages of sin (death) in all its forms came along with it.

Graciously, the loss of authority because of one man sinning in the garden was restored by Jesus, who was not touched by sin.

Consequently, just as one trespass resulted in condemnation for all people, so also one righteous act resulted in

> *justification and life for all people.*
> *For just as through the disobedience of the one man*
> *the many were made sinners,*
> *so also through the obedience of the one man*
> *the many will be made righteous.*
> (Romans 5:18–19)

Weed Seeds

So, although you are completely righteous in the eyes of God, nothing can separate you from His love, and sin no longer separates you from Him when you receive His grace, sin (yours and other peoples) still has the ability to influence your reality.

A great example of how sin still influences your reality is found in the analogy of a garden. When you receive the grace of God and your sins are forgiven, you are given a clean slate. In essence, the garden of your life becomes freshly tilled and open to receive the seeds of blessing that God has for you.

Sin has its own seed as well, and when you sow the seeds of sin into the garden of your life, they also produce their own fruit like weeds in your garden. Many times these weeds choke out things in your life that God wants for you.

This is why you can be completely forgiven and completely loved by God but still experience events that would not seem consistent with what the Bible says is His will or His promises for your life. The fruit of sin is still death. It's true that the choice to sin doesn't separate us from God, but sin still produces its fruit in our lives, and that fruit hurts us!

As stated in an earlier chapter, many of us assume when something bad happens that it's just God's will being manifested in our life, that we are being punished, or that He is trying to drive us into submission by the use of pain. I used to believe this was the case myself; however, the more I weigh circumstances through the lenses of God's love, the more convinced I am that when many bad things happen, it is simply the fruit of man (you, me, or someone else) using his God-given authority to choose sin instead of God's way of doing things . . . and the fruit of those decisions simply counteract blessings in our lives by stealing, killing, and destroying what God really intends and desires for His people.

What Will You Choose?

God is good and He loves you. He doesn't want bad things to happen to you, and He's not looking for ways to make them happen to teach you a lesson. He knows that sin has a way of robbing you of what He intends for you, and as a result, He has given you His Word, His grace, and His authority to be able to overcome all the power of the enemy!

Every day we face battles and choices. You can choose God's way (which includes His provision) or not. But whatever way you choose will produce a harvest in the garden of your life.

> *I call Heaven and Earth to witness against you today: I place before you Life and Death, Blessing and Curse. Choose life so that you and your children will live. And love GOD, your God, listening obediently to him, firmly embracing him.*
> *Oh yes, he is life itself.*
> (Deuteronomy 30:19–20 MSG)

Ultimately the choice is yours. So what will you choose?

Chapter 14

You Are Who He Says You Are

It's so easy to come up with reasons why we are not good enough or worthy of God's love. All most of us have to do is look in the mirror or spend more than a minute buying into the lies that our enemy fills our head with every day to feel unworthy. This is why it's vitally important that we don't define ourselves by what we see, but rather by the truth of what God's Word says about who we are.

There's always an element of truth in the lies that the enemy tries to sell us. It's true that we do make mistakes, we wouldn't be worthy part from Christ, and sin did separate us from God. But grace changed everything! I recently heard someone say, "Grace is not a thing, it is a person . . . and that person is Jesus."

Once we enter into relationship with God, our spirits are made alive in Christ, our sin is covered by the grace of God through the sacrifice of His Son, Jesus, and we become completely made new. We are no longer defined by the labels we received when we were lost, bound by our sin, and separated from God. The old you is gone, and everything that your previous sin defined you by is obliterated!

You Are Who God Says You Are

"So, who am I?" you might ask. The answer is simple: you are who God says you are! You are in right standing and completely justified in the eyes of God. You are more than a conqueror and are not defined by anything other than Jesus Himself (especially your past or even present sins). You are created in the image of God, given complete authority on the earth, and commissioned to use your God-given authority to be all that God created you to be.

You have a personal relationship with a loving God that no one and nothing can take away from you. What you have done or what has been done to you is forgiven and forgotten, and you are a completely new creation. You are not condemned. You need not fear judgment or be concerned about whether or not you are accepted by God—you are completely accepted by Him! You are not inadequate because every area where you may have been broken or imperfect is renewed and made perfect by the grace and love of God.

Isn't it funny how much we want to please God but often fall short in our own estimation and then beat ourselves up incessantly? This is because we haven't really embraced grace to the point that we believe it. It's like we *want* to believe that God is that good and would love us that much, but inside we still want to feel like we have earned it. So let me share a perspective that blew my mind when I first heard it.

**Jesus didn't become sin by *doing* sin,
and you don't become righteous by *doing* righteousness.**

Jesus was sinless and yet became sin for us, receiving and taking on our sin. In the same way, we who were unrighteous became righteous, not by being righteous, but by receiving and taking on His righteousness.

I'm convinced that people who have carried sin consciousness do so because they genuinely desire to please God. People who embrace the grace of God, the *true* grace of God, aren't looking for a way to justify sin so they can sin some more (as many have wrongly assumed). On the contrary, they have come to the understanding that they are no longer defined by their sin and are loved in spite of it, and this freedom in their understanding changes their perception of who God is and who they are to God, and ultimately creates an environment where they can grow without guilt always making them feel unworthy.

See Yourself Like God Sees You

Fear, condemnation, guilt, and self-loathing create a mentality where sin consciousness is your only reality. If perception determines reception, these mind-sets make it difficult to receive anything from God because you don't feel like you deserve it. And subsequently, you continue to live a life that is less than what God intended for you because, in your own mind, you are not truly right in God's eyes. Then your actions follow what you believe when you behave as though you are less than God says you are.

Those who know that they are loved by God, are called according to His purpose, and are no longer defined by what they do but who Christ is see themselves as forgiven. They believe that they are who God's Word says they are. These people simply live and respond differently to the lies of the enemy.

They carry themselves with the confidence of a child who knows he is loved in spite of his mistakes. They aren't looking to justify sin; they simply understand that sin is not what defines them, and they act like it. They don't have to tell me or anyone else what they believe; their actions show the world. And the Bible says that those who truly know their God are strong and do great things (Daniel 11:32).

It's so important that you discover who God says you really are in His Word and then adopt that image of yourself. The Bible says, "As [a man] thinks in his heart, so is he" (Proverbs 23:7 NASB). Wouldn't it be a shame if you had a million dollars in the bank and starved to death because you didn't know it was there? Yet this is what so many people do—they never become all that God created them to be because they believe a lie and never really embrace who they are in Christ.

You are who God says you are. Now, whether you believe it will determine if you ever become it.

So where does that leave you and what are you going to do about it?

Part III

Where Have I Been?

"If you haven't directly dealt with strongholds in your life, then you are likely dealing with strongholds in your life." I've shared this quote for years in churches. The truth is, whether you have been a Christian for a week or for fifty years, if you haven't been intentional in addressing and dealing with strongholds, then your past (where you have been and what you have experienced) has most certainly created opportunities for strongholds to be established and to grow.

Our past is probably the most fertile breeding ground for the continued dominance of strongholds. These strongholds have deep roots because they've been growing (and many times even nurtured) for a long time in the garden of your life.

How many times have you been doing great, getting ahead, feeling good about yourself, feeling good about your relationship with God, and then—*boom!*—you fell into the same trap you always fall into? It's not like you didn't see it coming. The attack was likely identical to what it was last time, and yet you found yourself almost powerless against it, even after promising God the last time that you'd never do it again. This is evidence that Satan has been able to establish a stronghold in your life to place a ceiling on your progress.

Usually, at a young age, something (or a sequence of things) happens that shapes how you process life, God, yourself, and other people. The enemy makes sure to capitalize on the pain in these seasons by encouraging you to erect walls of protection and unhealthy coping mechanisms that are the foundation for the strongholds (areas of control that are rooted in how we think, process, and act) to grow. Then a move at a time, like a lifelong chess match, the enemy uses additional events to increase the strength of the stronghold so that by the time you are reading this book, you have found yourself out of control in this arena of your life.

A stronghold can be anything that we find ourselves doing by default as a response to a specific catalyst, even when we don't want to and particularly when we feel pain. Satan convinces us to do these things in order to make us feel better, but in truth, most often we find ourselves feeling worse, more alienated, more used, and more distant from God and who we want to be as His child.

I think the ultimate purpose in Satan establishing this stronghold in your life is to keep you from ever going beyond the level where you become a threat to him. But where you have been does not have to control where you are or where you are going any longer. In part III of this book, we are going to address how today can be different from yesterday so that tomorrow can be better than today.

Chapter 15

Open Doors and Permission

Your past definitely influences the lenses that you view life through, while also affecting how you respond to temptation, and to what degree the enemy has a hold in your life. As we stated in a previous chapter, the Bible describes our enemy, Satan, as an angel of light (2 Corinthians 11:14); the one who deceived the whole earth (Revelations 12:9); the thief who comes to steal, kill, and destroy (John 10:10); and a roaring lion roaming the earth looking for someone to devour (1 Peter 5:8). Understanding all of these characteristics of our enemy can help us better confront and combat the one that has intentionally made life so difficult for us.

In this chapter, I'd like to address the first of two areas (permission and intrusion) where the doors of our lives often become open to attack and the enemy has the capacity to come in and set up camp in our house.

Permission

As we've established, it is inarguable from a biblical perspective that God loves you and His grace covers you. But if it's God's will that good things happen, and that He has great plans for your life, and that He lives within you and His promises are yours, then how is it that the Devil still has a place of authority in your life? I think the first reason and explanation often is that you've given him the permission to be there.

I recently heard the following quote from Kimberly Jones Pothier (aka Real Talk Kim): "Did the Devil really steal your joy or did you tell him he could hold it until God let you have your way?" Sometimes Satan comes in and blindsides us with an attack that puts us on our back, but many times we open the door to his influence through our conscious choices and in essence give him permission when we willfully sin and chose not to directly address things that we know are out of alignment with the will of God for our lives.

If God has given us a free will to choose whether we will do things His way or our way (sin's way), wouldn't it make sense that if we choose sin (and the wages of sin produce death), then our current reality may very well be shaped by the choices we've made of our free will?

It's as if God has given you a house and that house has multiple entry points (a front door, a back door, windows, etc.). There are several ways your enemy could gain entry into your house, but the easiest would be if he knocked on the front door and you gave him permission to come in. Of course, if he were dressed like the enemy (or how you'd expect the Devil to dress), you would slam the door in his face. But for many believers, our enemy came knocking with his good clothes on. He didn't come as a burglar dressed in all black, wearing a mask while looking to sneak in through a back door or a window; he came as a good-looking and smoothly dressed salesman—an angel of light and a deceiver.

Typically, the sale is delivered softly, with a lot of wiggle room. "It's not going to cost you much and it feels good to give in a little." "Everyone at your school has bought in and they are enjoying what I'm selling with no side-effects." "Every teenager in your youth group is doing it, and even if there is an additional cost, it's really minor and grace covers it." "It's just a little compromise." "Even the adults at church sin a little and their lives are just fine."

Once you have bought what he is selling, once you have believed the lie, you have empowered the liar with your permission. And there are always many attachments in the fine print that he didn't tell you about when you agreed to the initial terms of the sale. He's a fast talker, a methodical presenter, and quite capable of anticipating and disarming your arguments even before you present them. He knows that if you will give him permission, the seed of what he is selling will grow on its own. He just has to get it planted.

Open Doors and Permission

The way we often justify giving our permission is by calling our sins something less serious, like a "white lie," a "little sin," or to justify it by saying we are doing something noble, like protecting someone else, or excusing it by blaming someone for our actions, "I wouldn't be doing this if my parents would just be fair and not be so controlling." "I wouldn't have to lie or sneak around to cover up what I'm doing if Mom and Dad would give me the same freedom they give my older brother." "It's not really a big deal; everybody at school is doing this, and if Mom knew I lied she would be upset."

And so it goes. It starts small, but the "white lie" ends up having to be supported by another lie and another in order to save face. The "little sin" snowballs as excuses and complacency compound it into a sin that is bigger more and more difficult to handle. The thing you hid to protect someone from pain now has resulted in more and more hiding. And the seemingly harmless lie that you told your parents to keep from getting in trouble because you thought they were being unfair got you in a situation where you needed their help but were in so deep that it seems impossible to tell them now.

What You Tolerate You Authorize to Exist

My pastor often says, "What you tolerate, you authorize to exist," or in other words, if you do nothing to stop something, you give it permission by default.

So what sin in your life have you continued to excuse as "not a big deal"? What lie have you bought into that you thought would never amount to anything? Where did the enemy gain access into your life by your permission? Determining this helps to pinpoint the origin of entry and will help you better confront and overcome the sin fallout and subsequent strongholds that have been established in your life as a result. Identifying the point of origin gives us clarity to acknowledge how we initially gave the sin permission to enter our lives and provides us insight for the future when we are faced with similar choices.

Strongholds are rarely transplanted into our lives as full-grown mature weeds. On the contrary, most often they start as seemingly inconsequential seeds of compromise. But the choice for compromise leads to additional choices that actually morph into a habit or lifestyle of compromise that waters and cultivates the stronghold and allows it to take deeper root. If we had been able to see the full-grown weed (the end result) of the initial seed of compromise, we may have chosen differently—and that is the deception. Your enemy knew all along what it would produce in your life.

The great thing is this: even if you did give the enemy permission to set up camp in your life (whether you were deceived into it or you blatantly chose to do what was wrong), you can use the same authority you used to give him permission to evict him! It's still your house. He doesn't own it—you do! No matter how long he's been there, he doesn't have squatters' rights, and you don't have to give him any notice before eviction!

Throughout the remaining chapters we will be exposing these mind-sets and the necessary steps of acknowledging, addressing, and kicking out the unwanted guests.

Chapter 16

Open Doors Part II—Intrusion, Trespassing, and Invasion

In the previous chapter we discussed how our enemy gains access to our lives through permission by knocking on the door and as an angel of light and a deceiver, presenting an amazing sales pitch to get us to allow him access. In that situation, we have actually placed our agreement in the lie or deception he was selling and we chose to compromise. But there is another open door I'd like to address in which the flip side of Satan's personality becomes equally impacting and often more devastating in his effects when we don't know how to process the attack properly. It's called intrusion, and this is when he comes as a thief and a lion. We don't choose to let him in, but he forces his way in through another means with the intent to kill, steal, and destroy.

The number of areas where the enemy has tried to gain access to your life through intrusion are likely as vast as the number of those reading this book. But for clarity, *intrusion* is any event that happened *to* you and had the capacity to open the door for the enemy to gain access to your mind, change your lenses, and influence how you processed life after that point.

Maybe your parents divorced, or you were molested as a child. Perhaps you were verbally abused by a loved one, or someone in authority told you that you were stupid and would never amount to anything. Maybe you witnessed something tragic, you had a bad car accident, you were abandoned as a child, you were raped, your father is a drug addict, your mother exposed you to harmful relationships, you have been bullied by your peers for being overweight, or an authority figure lied to you. Whatever the case, something out of your control impacted you in ways that have been difficult to get past and overcome.

Intrusion, trespassing and invasion are responsible for so many of our insecurities and unhealthy mental habits. Because of these events (often happening a long time ago), you look in the mirror and label yourself with words that completely contradict who the Word of God says you are. Words like *failure, ugly, worthless, broken, used up, tainted, unwanted, unlovable, fat, irreparable, and undesirable* plague your mind.

So many of us find our identity in the tragedy and adopt the labels that accompany it. Even though it wasn't our fault, somehow we find a way to take responsibility and blame ourselves for what happened.

If I had been a better kid, my parents wouldn't have divorced.

If I had not gone to that place that day, I would not have encountered that tragedy.

If I had been more loveable and faithful to God, He would not have punished me by allowing this thing to happen.

Through this processing, we feel that we become somehow responsible for our own victimization and oftentimes God's will becomes the coconspirator in our tragedy.

You Are Not a Victim

But that's not true. Although you were *victimized*, you are not defined as a *victim*! Your enemy would like you to see yourself as less than others because of what has happened to you, but those labels are lies from the Devil that are designed to keep you from ever believing that you can be who God says you are. If you believe you are defined by your past, then you will not believe you are defined by God. And when you believe the lie about yourself, you empower the liar over your life.

Open Doors Part II—Intrusion

It is the thief, Satan, who comes to steal, kill, and destroy, but Jesus said that He has come that we might experience abundant life. The Devil would like you to believe that God was complicit in your tragedy because if he can get you to believe that God is abusive, then you aren't likely to ever truly trust Him. When you serve God out of fear, you don't exercise faith. If you don't believe that God is for you, then you won't seek Him as your helper when the enemy attempts to derail your destiny. Remember, without faith it's impossible to fully agree with God, and as we said in earlier chapters, *perception determines reception.* What you perceive about yourself, God, or your circumstances determines how you will respond to them!

The Attack Was Planned

The intrusion you experienced in your life was an absolutely intentional attack of your enemy in an attempt to establish a lifelong stronghold in your mind. Any time you begin to approach a season of advancement, he can use the event to once again create a ceiling for your progress.

Think about it: How many times has that event robbed you of your peace or kept you from pursuing greater things because of the mind-sets and labels you adopted as a direct result of what happened to you? Do you see that when you do this you have accepted a lie and placed your agreement in the lie? From this perspective, it's so blatantly obvious that this has been a huge and elaborate plan to keep you from being who God created you to be by placing your faith and agreement in blatant lies instead of the truth of what God says about you.

It's time to take back the ground that the Devil has taken from you. The things you believe, extend your faith toward, and place your agreement in have tremendous power to influence your life. Remember, the Bible says, "As [a man] thinks in his heart, so is he" (Proverbs 23:7 NLT). It's time to place your agreement in the truth of God's Word and what He says about you, instead of the trash your enemy is trying to sell you.

It's time to say, "No more!"

Say it out loud right now: "No more!"

Accept that you are God's child, loved by and defined by Him. You are not defined by what has happened to you. Even though it has influenced many things in your life and may have been the catalyst for poor decisions you have made or permissions you have given, that event is only a part of your story. It's not who you are! Thank God that even though you have been stolen from, God promises to restore the years that were stolen from you (Joel 2:25).

He is a great God, and He has a great plan for you. It's not too late. As a matter of fact, it's never too late. If you have air in your lungs, you can take back control of your life and your tomorrow can be better than your yesterday!

Chapter 17

The Infection of Rejection

There is an innate desire in human beings to feel loved, to belong, and to feel like they are contributing to the whole of society. If you plan to take psychology 101 in college, you'll learn about Maslow's Hierarchy of Needs.[3] Abraham Maslow, an American psychologist, wanted to understand what motivates people. He believed that people possess a set of motivation systems unrelated to rewards or unconscious desires. In 1943, he stated that people are motivated to achieve certain needs. When one need is fulfilled, a person seeks to fulfill the next one, and so on. This explains that our confidence, self-esteem, and ultimately whether or not we end up becoming who we were created to be rests upon how we process love and belonging. It would make sense that a significant attack our enemy would bring against our souls (mind, will, and emotions) would be in the form of rejection if he were attempting to keep us from becoming who God intended for us to be.

At some point rejection has infected your existence and impacted the lenses through which you viewed yourself and others, and quite possibly life as a whole. These things that happened to you (intrusions) became the catalyst for the stronghold of rejection setting in.

Because of an innate desire for love and belonging, when we feel rejected it causes us to question our value and our worth, and plants seeds of insecurity that often produce the fruit of

---

[3] http://www.simplypsychology.org/maslow.html.

various strongholds in our lives. Rejection is a significant catalyst for the establishment of other strongholds in the lives of believers and one that must be exposed and overcome with right thinking.

When you look back over your life, the mistakes you have made, and the choices that have influenced your current reality, ask yourself, "How many of these negative choices are directly connected to how I view myself or how I believe others view me?" If you truly believed that you had value, would you have made the decisions you made? Would you have tried to cope with your pain and emotions by using drugs or alcohol? Would you have used sex to find a sense of intimacy, belonging, or worth? Would you have hidden behind a mask of anger and violence to keep people from viewing you as weak? Would you have been so intentional to control every situation and person in your life so as not to get hurt again? Only you know, but the answers to these types of questions are likely "probably not."

Interestingly enough, once people have adopted these perspectives, a great many times they begin to process God through the same negative lenses. And through those lenses our enemy convinces us that not only are we *not valued* by others, but we are also rejected by God.

The Strategy
What a strategic move! Satan manipulates how we think through a series of negative experiences and then convinces us to turn away from the One who can change our situation and make all things new—our loving Father, the Creator of the universe, the one who promises never to leave us or forsake us, our amazingly compassionate God! And when he does that, we find ourselves bound and manipulated by the subsequent strongholds (many times for a lifetime) because, for fear and rejection, we simply never came to the knowledge of the truth that would set us free.

God, in our minds, becomes part of the poison of our process. He becomes another point of pain. The rejection we feel becomes compounded because in our minds we weren't good enough for anyone else and now even God has turned His back on us—when He of all people was supposed to love us when no one else does.

The Infection of Rejection

Just like water is essential for life, when it comes to freedom from strongholds, seeing ourselves as God truly sees us is essential to overcoming. Yet many of us have been told by the enemy that the "water" is poison and will kill us. Then, as a result, we die of thirst when it's not the water that is poisonous, but the lie we believed about it!

You Are Not Rejected by God

To God you are not the black sheep, the exception to the rule of His love, or the outsider in the family. God placed you on this planet at this exact moment for a purpose that you will only fulfill when you are walking in the fullness of who He created you to be in Him. You may have been unplanned by your family, but you were not unplanned by God. The Bible says that He knew you before you were ever formed in your mother's womb and He had a plan for you.

Even if you have felt unwanted or unappreciated, your amazing God wants you and loves you beyond measure. He laughs when you laugh; He weeps when you hurt. He cheers when you win. He wants you to become that thing you have dreamt about being since you were a child more than you do. As a matter of fact, He is the one who placed that desire in you in the first place.

You are who He says you are. You are the perfect you that He created you to be, and if you don't know it in your heart yet, you will as you open your soul to hear and accept His voice. He speaks the truth to your heart, even when your mind says otherwise.

Ask Him today to show you a picture of yourself through His eyes. Close your eyes and do it now. Ask God to show you a picture of yourself from His perspective. Ask Him to let you feel how He feels about you.

God loves you! The Bible is filled with clear definitions of how much He loves and accepts you. You may have been rejected by family members, leaders, or friends, but you are not rejected by God. You are not defined by the pain or the choices of your past. He sees you only through eyes of love, grace, and acceptance. There may even have been pastors who attempted to manipulate you by teaching that God rejected you in hopes that you would choose different behaviors if you feared God's disapproval. They were wrong to do that, and they were wrong about what they said. You are not rejected by God. You are cherished by Him.

Now the question becomes this: Are you willing to place your agreement in His image of you, even if His perspective differs from what you have been told or agreed with in the past?

Chapter 18

Processing the Pain

Few things have the ability to dominate our thoughts like pain. When you are in pain it is difficult to focus on anything other than the pain, and depending on the severity of it, many will resort to any means necessary to eliminate it!

I often become frustrated when I hear someone who has not experienced intense pain tell someone who is in the midst of it to "Get over it," like they have any idea what the other person is dealing with. If it were only that easy, they would have "gotten over it" a long time ago!

I'm also convinced that the person who came up with the saying, "When life gives you lemons, make lemonade," was never dealt a rotten lemon. For those of us who have been, there is no amount of sugar that can sweeten the taste of the rotten lemon to make it palatable. So what do we do when our lives have been molded by a rotten-lemon experience?

The first step is acknowledging the legitimacy of the pain. That painful experience has played a huge role in your current reality. You are not weak because you feel hurt and pain. And you are not broken because you cannot forget. As I said before, pain has a way of capturing our focus. Only you can assess the level of the pain, and no one else (or their expectations) can set the bar for how you process it.

Don't Accept the Labels

The pit that I believe many young adults fall into as a result of their pain is that they accept the labels and lies that are often associated with the pain. Do you believe that you are permanently broken? Do you think that you are an unrepairable victim? If so, then you have likely adopted a mode of operation that is consistent with the victim mentality we discussed in previous chapters. As long as you see yourself primarily through the eyes of weakness and victimization, you will likely respond as the victim, and this mind-set will impact every relationship in your life. Yes, the pain you've endured is a part of your life's story, but that event (or sequence of events) does not define you! Just because it happened to you does not mean that is who you are! So don't allow the "victim" to be a major part of what defines you in your eyes or anyone else's.

A few years ago a close friend asked me why I hated weakness in myself so much and strived so hard to maintain the warrior image I projected. He asked me if I was a mamma's boy when I was a child and then asked me if I had been molested. I was so angry with his questions because, although I had hidden it my whole life, when I was a child I cried easily, I was afraid of everything, and yes, I had been molested. I came to hate that softness, and I viewed it as weakness. So as I grew up, I overcompensated to the point where I despised even a hint of weakness in myself or anyone else.

When my friend asked me those questions, I wanted to run away! I wanted to lash out. Every part of me wanted to change the subject. But I knew he was right. I did hate weakness, especially in myself. And I answered him honestly, saying, "Yes, I was molested and I was a mamma's boy. I cried easily as a child. If another kid got yelled at, I would get nervous and get emotional. I was soft-natured."

My friend followed up with another series of questions. "Aaron, do you believe that God created you as that sweet-natured child who was in touch with his feelings, felt compassion, and felt emotion?"

I had to agree that God had likely created me that way. His next question floored me. "Aaron, then who do you think God would be more likely to use: the you *He created* or the you that *you have created*?" I had to admit I had never considered that thought before.

Processing the Pain

My friend went on to say, "Aaron, you are the sum total of who God created you to be and your life's experiences. But as long as you fight the softness that God created you to possess so you could feel compassion and empathy, you will never be the complete leader you were created to be. You are created to be the Mamma's Boy Warrior. Like King David, the harp player and giant slayer, or Jesus Himself, who was moved with compassion by the needs of people, unless you embrace that mamma's boy, you'll never really find a place of fulfillment in your life's pursuits!"

Standing there with my friend, I realized I had adopted a label of victimization. Because I was soft-natured and cried easily, because the other kids made fun of me for crying, and because I was ashamed of the molestation, I adopted a self-image of being weak, even broken. Then, because I refused to continue to be weak, I did everything I could to become some distorted version of strong that I adopted along the way. I so deeply hated being the kid that the other children laughed at for crying that I spent most of my life suppressing emotion, doing that which I feared until I wasn't afraid anymore, and destroying the image of weakness in myself by lifting weights, getting strong, projecting an image of toughness, and not allowing people to walk on me.

As a result, strongholds of false pride, self-assurance, self-reliance, and arrogance (all rooted in fear) set in to compensate for what I believed was wrong with me. The truth was, I was just a kid who had experienced hurt and carried that pain into my adulthood. The pain was real, but the label I adopted was not!

Overcoming the Pain

No matter the source of the pain, there's no denying that it has influenced you, but it's vital to realize that it has not defined you. Overcoming pain does not begin with denying the pain; it begins by denying the labels. For some, the labels can be as diverse as the lenses we have developed to deal with them. To this day, I still discover new lenses that I have developed to process pain and insecurity I didn't even realize were there.

Occasionally someone will say something that will surprise me and make me angry. Through intentional self-evaluation study, and teaching classes related to processing labels and the lenses that accompany them, I've learned to intentionally ask myself, *Why is this impacting me this way?* Or, *What about this thing had the power to influence my emotions on this scale?* The answer most often exists in what I have accepted, believed, or agreed with pertaining to how I view myself (especially as it pertains to the lies I have agreed with over my lifetime). The lie we buy, as it relates to pain, is most often exaggerated by what we accept as the truth. Once I identify the lie I have accepted, I then counter it with the truth about that scenario presented in God's Word.

You are the sum total of who God created you to be combined with your life experiences. God didn't necessarily *will* bad stuff to happen to you, nevertheless, it happened. Still, God can work all things together for our good if we allow Him to, and I'm convinced that it's because He's not content to allow tragedy to be the last word in your life. And as long as you are not content for it to be, I don't believe it has to be.

When God's Word says that you can do all things through Christ, He meant it. Now the question is, will you believe it?

Chapter 19

100 Percent

Sometimes when you have experienced a lot of pain, seeing yourself as a victor is difficult. But let me put something in perspective for you: you've already made it through 100 percent of your worst days in life!

There are very few things that carry a 100-percent statistic, so that victorious statement is extremely significant. I realize that many of those days don't feel like victories, but they are. They were intended to destroy you, they were sent to take you out, they were planned to be the death of you . . . yet you are still here.

As I mentioned earlier, on the last day of my career as a detective and SWAT team member, two young men tried to kill me. I could have processed it as a significant loss (and initially I did). I mean, after all, I was a good cop. In the years preceding my medical retirement, I had been awarded Officer of the Year and had been recruited by the Tennessee State Police to be a training officer for their DARE program. I worked hard, I went through every training opportunity I could, and I was certified in everything they would allow me to be. Just a few months before I was attacked, I was offered a job with the Tennessee Bureau of Investigation (TBI) as an investigator with the state. They even offered to pay for me to go back to college so that I would meet the educational prerequisites necessary if I would just come to work for them.

When I was forced into retirement by the doctors, I didn't receive any compensation because I live in a "Right to Work" state, which means that my employer didn't have to provide me with a pension. When I lost my job, I lost everything I had worked for and had nothing to show for it. I lost my job (and every opportunity connected to it), my health insurance, and my personal business. Then the economy tanked, and I couldn't get a job for years. To date, the injuries have cost me nearly a million dollars in lost wages.

You Choose Your Focus

I could be bitter. I could walk around feeling like a victim who was unfairly wronged. I could reflect negatively on a system that failed me when I gave them my best. But I don't.

That's not to say I haven't had to deal with difficult feelings and emotions. After my accident, I went through a significant depression. I felt like a failure. I've reflected back on some very unfair situations and not known how to process them. I've cried. I've been angry. I've experienced normal emotions over the course of nearly a decade, but I've come to realize that I have the power to choose how I allow myself to define me and how I respond to the circumstances I've encountered.

I refuse to be defined as the victim! Being victimized and wronged is a part of my experience, but it is not the label I will allow to be stuck on my forehead for everyone to read. I win because I made it through everything I encountered. I was nearly killed (and many officers that year were), but I wasn't. I was nearly destroyed financially, but I'm still here and somehow we always had food to eat and a bed to sleep on. I was devastated emotionally, which impacted me psychologically for a season, but I'm back and better than ever. The enemy intended to crush me with these circumstances, and I might have been crushed if I had allowed myself to adopt the label that was projected upon me in that season, but I refuse to agree with and see myself through those lenses.

On days when my world was literally spinning out of control with severe 24/7 vertigo, I would stand in the middle of my living room and raise my hands toward heaven and say out loud, "Yet will I trust You!"

Those were dark, lonely, difficult, painful days . . . and they lasted for a few years. I would have a few good days, then a few bad days when I found myself struggling with where to place my agreement, then a few more good days. In time, the good days were more and more, and the bad days were less and less.

This Too Shall Pass

I remember during the darkest time, my dad said to me, "Son, I know this is really hard right now, but I promise you, it will get better and this too shall pass." I clung to those words during the bad days and you know what? He was right! It got better. I chose in that time to surround myself with people who positively impacted my life. I was very intentional not to focus on negative things. I read inspirational materials. I listened to music and programming that didn't project negativity into my life.

Isn't it funny how natural it seems to put on a sad song when we are depressed? I chose in that season to intentionally not do that kind of stuff. I spent a lot of time writing and blogging. When I wrote I would write from the perspective of what I would say to someone who was going through what I was experiencing. The Bible says that David encouraged himself in the Lord (1 Samuel 30:6 KJV), and many days that was exactly what I did.

It wasn't always easy and some days were much more difficult than others, but I made it through 100 percent of the dark days. At times I wanted to throw in the towel. At times I wanted to quit. At times I wanted to give in, but I chose to move forward even if it was an inch at a time.

I remember one particularly hard day when my world was spinning from severe vertigo. In tears and emotionally tapped, I turned to my wife and said, "I never want to waste another day." I was determined to get through it. It was a conscious choice to pursue whatever it would take to win. I refused to be defined as a victim and I refused to allow the Devil to steal one more day of my life. And so can you!

In the Bible there is a command that a thief must payback seven times what he has stolen:

> *But when he (a thief) is found,*
> *he must repay seven times [what he stole];*
> *He must give all the property of his house*
> *[if necessary to meet his fine].*

Aaron D. Davis

(Proverbs 6:31 AMP)

So if someone was victimized or stolen from and the thief was caught, he was responsible to repay seven times more than he had stolen as punishment for stealing. I've heard it taught that there are spiritual parallels for this as well, that when the Devil steals from us we can demand that God restore more than what was taken from us. Even Job (who lived under a completely different and inferior covenant compared to what we do today because of Jesus) received double in return for what was taken from him.

In my life, for a period of time, I saw myself as a victim. As a victim, if I were to use this scripture I could place a demand on the thief and expect that the return be greater than was taken from me. But then I had another epiphany of sorts. You see, there is another set of scriptures in the Bible that says that when we sow something in seed form (invest it into the kingdom of God), then the return is thirtyfold, sixtyfold, and a hundredfold!

And the one on whom seed was sown on the good soil, this is the one who hears the word and understands and grasps it; he indeed bears fruit and yields, some a hundred times [as much as was sown], some sixty [times as much], and some thirty.
(Matthew 13:23 AMP)

When I read that about the sowers (investors) return, something clicked in my heart and it hit me: Maybe this is why the Bible says if someone takes your coat, give them your shirt too. Maybe it's about refusing to be a victim so that the return on your investment will be exponentially higher than sevenfold.

God is always faithful, and if I *choose* to be defined as a victim, I can still demand a victim's return. But if I want to see myself as God sees me and I choose to sow my pain and difficulty and experiences into the kingdom of God and allow God to shape me and mold me through those experiences, not as a victim, but as an overcomer training for high-level leadership, then the return on my investment is multiplied exponentially thirty, sixty, and one hundred times!

Even though it wasn't fair and I didn't deserve it, I chose then and choose now to allow God to take it and use it. I'm not going to be a victim. I'm not going to walk around with a pitiful mental perspective. I was created with limitless potential, as you were. I'm a child of the King, as are you. I was wronged, but He made me better in spite of it, and He'll make you better too.

The Label You Embrace Will Define You

So now it's your choice. How will you define your experiences? Victory begins with deciding if you will allow yourself to be defined as a victim or a victor. What are you willing to agree with? What label are you willing to embrace? The label you embrace will define you. Are you going to press through and overcome the lies of your past that try to falsely define you? Or are you going to lie down, accept them, and wallow in them? How you see yourself will ultimately be how others see you and impact how they receive you.

If you choose to be defined as the victim, you will carry yourself, be received as, and be responded to as a victim. If you choose to see yourself as the victor God says you are, you will carry yourself confidently and will be received and responded to respectably and honorably as a victor.

I realize this is not always an easy choice to live out, but it begins with determining what you are not willing to be defined by. You can only begin to carry yourself as a winner when you refuse to allow yourself to be defined in your own mind as a loser. It may take a bit longer to actually see yourself as the victor and the winner that God says you are, but you will never get to that point as long as you are content with the label of a "victim" or defined as the loser.

What you become is most affected by what you are willing to accept or agree with. So the question becomes, what label will you choose to agree with?

Are you a victim or are you a victor? In the next chapters we will discuss how a victor overcomes the pain of the past.

Chapter 20

The Power of Words

"Sticks and stones can break my bones but words will never hurt me." As a child I can remember chanting that phrase when another child called me a name or made fun of me. Although designed to teach us not to allow the words of others to impact us, there is very little truth in the statement, because not only do words hurt—they actually contain power.

Proverbs 18:21 tells us that death and life are in the power of the tongue. Job 22:28 says that if we will declare a thing then it will be established. Jesus told us in Mark 11:22–23 that if we speak to a mountain while exercising just a small amount of faith, then the mountain will move. Even the confession of your mouth that "Jesus is Lord" is a solidifying factor outlined by Paul in Romans 10 for assuredness of salvation.

The Bible didn't say, "Declare a *good thing* and it would be established." It said, "Declare a thing and it would be established" (Job 22:28 NKJV). Words were designed by God to carry power, so even when negative words are spoken over us (by ourselves or others), something often takes root.

God used words and *spoke* nearly all of physicality into existence in Genesis 1. But not us. He created us with His hands, in His image, and breathed life into us! Unlike the rest of creation, He gave us His breath, and our words are the carriers through which we convey blessings or curses.

The Power of Words

Blessings and Curses

The Bible is very intentional to point out the importance of the words we speak because words have the power and the ability to influence environments and impact realities.

Many of you have already experienced the power of words when a classmate put you down or made fun of you. Some of you had an authority figure say something mean to you years ago, and yet those words still replay in your mind and stir emotions when you think about them. *That's because words have power.*

Blessings and curses are typically areas of misunderstood impact. With the ability to create and destroy, build up or tear down, encourage or discourage, words (and our agreement with them) are often the catalyst for many of our successes and failures. Words are also frequently a distinct source for the establishment of strongholds in your life.

Some of these destructive words (curses) have been spoken through parents, peers, and authority figures and taken root by wounding us and opening doors in our lives through *intrusion*. Others have been spoken into our lives with our own mouths and created undesired realities by our *invitation*.

As we stated in an earlier chapter, the Bible says in Proverbs 23:7 that a man becomes who he thinks in his heart that he is. It also says in Matthew 12:34 and Luke 6:45 that the words we speak reflect what we believe in our heart.

> *Guard your heart above all else,*
> *for it determines the course of your life.*
> (Proverbs 4:23 NLT)

Taking into account all of these biblical references about the heart and the direct influence that words (ours and others) have on it, it seems that we should be mindful of the words we allow to be spoken over us (or say ourselves) and those that we allow to take root in us.

I can hear some saying right now, "How can I control what others say or have said about me?" And the answer is, you can't. But as it pertains to the establishment of strongholds in your life through words, you have to develop an *aggressive attitude* toward declaring good things in your life, instead of placing your agreement in the curses of others by allowing the negative, faithless words of yesterday to impact your tomorrow.

I'm not necessarily saying to argue with a person who has spoken negative things over you. But you can mentally reject those labels and walk away. Many adults still struggle today with the words that were spoken over them when they were children. Just take a few moments and think about some of the most hurtful things people have said about you or to you. I'd be willing to bet that at least one instance of a hurtful event popped right into your mind. That's because we can carry these hurts for years just under the surface.

Imagine how your life might be different if you didn't believe these lies about yourself, even in the smallest way. Would you be more confident? Would you have better relationships with others? Would you have a closer relationship with God?

You Choose Whose Words You Will Adopt

As you can see, the issue becomes where we place our agreement today regarding the curses of yesterday. When we replay those words over and over in our minds and agree with those words by accepting them as truth, the power of those words becomes amplified. Phrases like "I'm fat," "I'm ugly," "I'm stupid," "I'll never be . . . (fill in the blank)" are self-destructive. Thankfully, it's never too late to begin to undo what has been negatively done by declaring positive, faith-filled confessions over yourself and agreeing with the truth of God's words about you instead of the lies attached to the curses you once accepted.

Remember, according to the Bible, not only is the power of death in the tongue, but so is life! Not only can you curse your reality and tear down your heart by agreeing with negative words and speaking them over your life, but you can guard your heart and bless your life with positive words as well.

When those negative words come to your mind and you are tempted to believe them or even repeat them about yourself, take a moment to reverse the curse and speak life. You choose whose words you will believe. You choose whose words you will adopt. You choose whose blessings or curses you agree with and influence your reality, and you choose how you allow yourself to be defined. You have the power to change things with your own words. It doesn't take away the sting of the words that have been spoken. Words hurt when they are used as weapons, but agreeing with God's Word and declaring faith-filled blessings over yourself does change whether or not you take on the label (or curse) attached to the negative declarations.

Sometimes, in the beginning, it's hard to believe the blessings and positive affirmations you are saying about yourself (especially when you believed something negative for so long). But as you put yourself in agreement with God and His words about you, and you extend your faith by speaking and agreeing with the truth of His Word, perceptions begin to change and your agreement with God's Word sparks a new belief system.

When those perceptions begin to change, you quit allowing yourself to be influenced by the lies spoken in the curses, and you put yourself in a position to receive the peace associated with the blessings that God declares for you and that you are now declaring over your own life.

What You Do Daily You Become Permanently

I'm sure some are asking right now, "What should I declare and how frequently should I be making these positive declarations?" I don't think the formula for success is in a specific number, but rather a consistent and persistent mind-set and intentionality that simply refuses to allow those negative thoughts to have a place to live and grow. What you do daily you become permanently.

The issues and strongholds you have dealt with in your life may be different from what I have had to confront. There are thousands of promises in the Bible relating to different things. A good idea would be to perform a study, looking up some positive and affirming scriptures to meditate on that directly relate to your struggles.

If you don't know what the Bible says about what you are dealing with, there is zero excuse for ignorance today. There has never been a time in history where you can discover information at a faster pace. With a few keystrokes on a computer or a trip to the local library, you can read pages and pages of detailed information directly relating to what you are pursuing to understand.

If you have difficulty with low self-esteem, or guilt, or anger, or lust, or depression, or pride—whatever your issue(s) is rooted in—do an Internet search looking up scriptures for that issue and write down those verses. Then do another search on "biblical promises," and write down those scriptures. Determine the ones that most closely relate to and encourage you, and then memorize them and put them on sticky notes around your house to remind you what God says about you throughout the day.

Then when the negative thoughts come in, you have the positive words already in your heart and mind, and you can immediately and intentionally contradict those lies with God's Words and thoughts about you. In those moments you can say, "No, I'm not that. I am who God says I am!"

Because death can be in the power of the tongue, we are absolutely negatively impacted by negative words spoken, so why would we not also be positively impacted by positive words spoken when life is also in the power of the tongue?

Speak positive words over yourself today. Reverse the curse with words of life! Don't buy the lie. Defy the lie and speak life!

Chapter 21

Curse Consciousness

Because bondage and strongholds associated with where we have been can have some deeper root causes from a biblical perspective, I would like to briefly address a few of these issues before we step into the next section of this book, "Where Am I Now?"

In this section I would like to present a term that I'm going to continue to use for the rest of this chapter: *curse consciousness*. As we have discussed before, what we believe or think about has the potential to influence our realities, and this is very true when it comes to how we process the topic of *curses* in our lives.

When you read the Bible, you may have seen terms referring to biblical examples of curses like generational curse, word curse, curses spoken over us by people involved in the occult, curses associated with participation in witchcraft, curses associated with gossiping and judgmental accusation, curses associated with ungodly sexual participation, curses from worshiping false Gods, curses associated from intentionally harming or taking advantage of the weak, curses associated with not doing what God has instructed with your money, and curses on your life from being disobedient and disrespectful to your parents.

The truth is, all of the behavioral patterns associated with these listed curses should not be reflective of how someone who has been transformed by the power of God and influenced by His Spirit now residing within them would behave after entering a relationship with Christ and being renewed by Him. These behaviors and the curses associated with them are a part of our unredeemed past, and they have been covered by the blood of Jesus! Many of these curses were outlined in the Old Testament (and under the old covenant) as a result of sinning against God, and of course, the blessings of God were also many times contingent upon not doing these things.

Because there is still a reaping and sowing principle attached to some of the things we have done, sin still has the power to produce death in our lives (before and after we become saved). For example, if I had sex with someone who had a sexually transmitted disease and I too contracted that disease, becoming or being a Christian wouldn't just erase the disease I contracted. (Although I don't rule out the possibility of becoming healed because Christ took our curses upon Himself, and I've seen many instances where God has miraculously healed people from sickness and disease.)

In the same way, I do not underestimate the power of negative (and even spiritually empowered) words and curses spoken against us as believers. Certainly there is ample evidence in the world and maybe in your own life where negative words and even associations have produced their own ungodly harvest. But I also am very intentional to not overemphasize the power of the Devil. Our God is bigger . . . and quite frankly, we win!

Still, what I see happen most frequently as a freedom minister is that, as people become more knowledgeable about the many types of curses that influence the lives of believers today, many adopt the mind-set attached to a curse from a previous season of their life and carry that mind-set into the next season through curse consciousness. In other words, they continue to see themselves bound in an area where Christ has set them free. When this happens to you, your internal reality becomes your external reality, and subsequently, you find yourself (and your thoughts) under the influence of generational sin or curses that Christ has given you victory over.

Therefore, if anyone is in Christ, he is a new creation; old things have passed away; behold, all things have become new.
(2 Corinthians 5:17 NKJV)

All Things New

All things have become new. The word *new* here is actually the Greek word *kainos*, which means "of a new kind, unprecedented, novel, uncommon, or unheard of." You have been made completely new in a way that transforms you into something that doesn't even resemble the old you; yet in freedom ministry I frequently see believers who have been made new in Christ still willing to operate under the strongholds of yesterday because they believe they have to.

A perfect example of this is when people say something like, "My grandfather had a terrible temper, my father had a terrible temper, and I have a terrible temper!" Or, "My grandmother was a nag, my mother was a nag, and I'm a nag." In essence, excuses are made for what has been wrong or cursed generationally as an aspect of "that's just who I am" and they have no confident expectation of good coming from the wrong or healing occurring because of the obstacle of curse consciousness. But operating under and living with these curses is an existence that is inferior to what Christ has provided for you . . . and life simply doesn't have to be lived that way!

Christ redeemed us from that self-defeating, cursed life by absorbing it completely into himself. Do you remember the Scripture that says, "Cursed is everyone who hangs on a tree"? That is what happened when Jesus was nailed to the cross: He became a curse, and at the same time dissolved the curse. And now, because of that, the air is cleared and we can see that Abraham's blessing is present and available for non-Jews, too. We are all able to receive God's life, his Spirit, in and with us by believing.
(Galatians 3:13–14 MSG)

Certainly, as in the case of generational sin, there are familiar patterns and behaviors (and perhaps even demonic spiritual influences) that have been a part of families and have been tolerated, nurtured, and granted permission to operate in the family for many years, decades even. And as a result, because of exposure to these patterns, they may have become a behavioral pattern that you have adopted. But you do not have to continue to give these familiar spirits (spiritual influences that have been tolerated in your family) permission to operate in *your life* or continue on in *your family legacy*.

The Curse Ends with Me

A few years before my son, Rocky, was born, I was in a season where I was coming to a place of understanding about who God is in my life and who I am as a result of being His son. I remember being in a church service where we were all declaring blessings out loud, repeating after the pastor when he said, "I am not defeated," "I am a child of God," and "I am who God says I am." In that moment of declaring, I shouted out, "The curse ends with me!" When I said it, I was overcome with emotion. Something clicked in me as the words passed my lips. I didn't have any children yet, but I was determining in that moment that I was not going to continue to be bound by things my grandfather and father dealt with, such as an uncontrollable anger and an abusive vocabulary, and my kids would not have to deal with the strongholds that I was given the authority to destroy in our family.

I believe that my grandfather loved his family. I'm convinced that if someone came into his home to hurt one of his children, he would have fought to the death to protect them. Yet, in spite of the love he had for his children, he sometimes operated in abusive ways with them that would be considered highly dysfunctional.

He experienced a very difficult life growing up. He was impacted by a mother who had likely experienced abuse as well and struggled with her own demons, which probably influenced her actions and lead her at times to be terribly abusive to my grandfather (by his account) and ultimately to abandon him.

These actions by my great-grandmother likely had a significant impact on my grandfather. Insecurities were most probably established in my grandfather because of the abuse he experienced. He likely struggled with feeling loved. He likely warred with feelings of inadequacy, and I'm quite confident that he overcompensated for these insecurities by building walls that would not allow for others to hurt him.

He was a massive and very strong man. Analyzing his behavior, he likely learned that between his size, strength, and temper, he could manipulate and control situations that as a child would have left him feeling completely out of control. Even though he loved big, there was another side to him that did not resemble love and was influenced and controlled by the puppet strings of the evil strongholds rooted in those childhood pains. As a result, he was himself at times abusive toward his family and made decisions that left others hurting.

It would be easy to say that because my grandfather had a temper and he passed that behavior on to my father (who thankfully chose to parent me in a kinder manner), I also could have a bad temper and blame it on genetics. But that would be a lie. I don't have to operate under that curse. And neither do you.

Self-Fulfilling Prophecy

When we accept or tolerate operating under the curse of what has always been, we will continue to live bound by it. In psychology this is called a *self-fulfilling prophecy*, which basically states, "What you believe will happen most often does." But when you understand you are free because Jesus really paid for you to be, you realize that there is no excuse or curse that is greater than the sacrifice that He made for you. And His blood is enough to cover every curse and transform us all!

What you have done, what you have observed in your family, what you have been taught to do and be, the curses that have been spoken over you, the intentional destructive events that the enemy brought into your life early on in your childhood to set a ceiling for your progress—these things can be overcome! In actuality, it *already has been overcome* by the blood of Jesus. You have to place your agreement in the truth in order to experience the movement of that curse consciousness mountain from an *obstacle* of your progress to a *spectacle* of the power of God!

Beloved, I pray that you may prosper in all things and be in health, just as your soul prospers.
(3 John 1:2 NKJV)

You Are Not Cursed

What you believe about who you are influences who you become. And the first step to walking outside of the effects of those lying curses is to understand and place your agreement in the fact that they are not acceptable to exist in your life! Third John 1:2 says that your health and your external prosperity happen when your soul prospers. What happens internally happens externally and shapes the reality you experience.

You are not cursed, you do not function under a curse, you are not destined to be cursed, and you are not defined by a curse! You are loved by God and called according to His purpose. You are wonderfully made and completely made new. There is no condemnation or accusation to be brought against you because you are a child of the God who created the universe.

Revelation 12:11 says, "They overcame by the blood of the Lamb, and by the word of their testimony" (KJV). It's the sacrifice of Jesus (the blood of the Lamb) freeing you from all the works of the Devil and your faith-filled agreement/declaration (word of your testimony—or declaration of your mouth testifying of its truth) that enable you to experience the limitless freedom power and potential that God created you for.

Do not be content to operate as less than who God says you are and who Christ paid a great price for you to be! Ask God to give you strength and wisdom to be able to see where you have agreed with behaviors, attitudes, and belief systems that are ungodly. Set your agreement and declaration in the truth of who God says you are. Determine that you will not agree (or declare) to be anything less than that which God has created you to be. Then when those behaviors try to rear their ugly faces (because they will), declare that Jesus has set you free from the negative words, curses, attitudes, actions, and agreements that have influenced your current reality. Release your faith to be more than you ever believed you could be before, and walk free from the curse!

For I can do everything through Christ, who gives me strength.
(Philippians 4:13 NLT)

Curse Consciousness

The word *everything* in this verse, translated from the original text means . . . everything!

Part IV

Where Am I Now?

Up to this point we've discussed who God is, who you are, and where you've been. You've been exposed to the inconsistencies between what the Bible says about these topics and what you may have personally experienced. So what do you need to understand in order to impact you today and help you continue to experience the limitless freedom, power, and potential that you were created for tomorrow?

In part IV, we are going to expose some of the greatest obstacles to your freedom and develop a game plan that you can begin implementing today to directly confront those obstacles. You can experience a *limitless* life that is free from the oppression of strongholds!

Chapter 22

Punching Puppets

By now there should be a revelation beginning to take place where you are able to see what issues the enemy—the puppet master—has used in your life to manipulate you. There have, of course, been many physical contributors to your *past* experiences as well as to your *current* realities, but not everything you've experienced has necessarily always been what it seemed.

Yes, *a person* may have harmed you, but when you see life through only the lens of physical world, you aren't able to fully process the reasoning behind what happened. Your physical lenses can only interpret a partial reality, because the physical realm is only a part of the whole.

We are all combating a common enemy, and not acknowledging him does not limit the effects of his attack. As a matter of fact, one of his biggest hopes is that you will not recognize that he is behind most of what you are fighting against and that the battle is actually spiritual instead of physical. In this arena, *what you don't know* might actually kill you!

The Bible tells us in Ephesians 6:12 that although our battles may appear physical, the fight actually takes place in the spirit realm against demonic enemies. They exist in other dimensions, and they are directly influencing what is happening in our physical lives.

It's vital to recognize that strongholds established in the lives of others also influences their behaviors in such a way that their problems can impact your current reality. So, yes, it was your mother or father or teacher or friend or coworker who hurt you, but processing outside of that box, ask yourself, "Is it possible that their actions were being influenced by their own strongholds and spiritual puppet master?"

For example: Let's go back to the story of my grandfather and his anger issues. His poor behavior caused a lot of damage to our family. Is my grandfather to blame? Yes. To a great extent, he is to blame for his choices and actions. But we need to recognize from a biblical perspective that our fight is not really against the physical, and there was a spiritual catalyst, a puppet master if you will, at work behind the scenes that greatly influenced the culture and dynamic of the entire Davis family. And my grandfather was probably never really completely aware of this spiritual catalyst.

It's not that my grandfather did not have a relationship with Jesus; he did. But I don't think anyone ever taught him how to cut the strings of the strongholds in his life. As a result, a lack of knowledge may have strengthened his poor behavior.

Choosing to Change

My grandfather was raised to behave and maybe even survive life events in a way that ended up influencing his children and even his children's children. My dad was raised by his father to embrace the stronghold of anger and rage like his father had. Grandpa taught my dad the only way that he knew as a means of survival and that was to be violent and feed the rage. But several years after I came along, my dad made the decision to change that legacy.

Until I was about seven or eight years old, my dad educated me in some of the "family ways." But then he decided that he would not raise me with the same dysfunctional anger, rage, and aggression that he had been raised with. Recognizing the long-term effects attached to those behaviors, he determined that he was not going to teach me to submit to the same evil spiritual influences that he and his father before him spent a lifetime warring against. And he began instructing me differently. I can still remember Dad sitting me down and explaining to me that he was wrong for some of what he had exposed me to, and he was going to do things differently with me than was done with him.

My dad determined that I would not be left to fight *his* demons, and he hit his knees in repentance (remember, *repentance* means to "change your mind"). He learned to think differently, put on the mind of Christ, place his agreement in God's Word, and subsequently to teach me, his son, to think and respond differently.

I can say with certainty that although I've had my own struggles with anger and rage, I do not struggle with them on the same scale as my father or his father before him did. I've certainly had to war with myself, and the enemy has most definitely given me the opportunity to embrace and feed this familiar influence over the course of my lifetime, but it's been undeniably different from what Grandpa or Dad struggled with.

Because of my father's choice to repent and take a stand against the spiritual forces at work in our family, I can look at my son and my two sisters' children, and I do not see anything resembling the emotional and spiritual dysfunction present in their great-grandfather. Our kids and their children will have their own spiritual battles (giants) to fight, but at least they will not have to fight their great-grandfather's giants.

Admit It, Quit It, Be It

There is so much to be gained from a clear perspective. When you can learn to see the spiritual puppet strings that are influencing the actions of those coming against you, then you can learn to combat the situation by fighting against the puppet master instead of just taking swings at the ignorant puppet.

Maybe you've been the puppet. Maybe you've developed strongholds in your life based upon the negative influence of other puppets who themselves were controlled by the strings of strongholds. You can learn to see people (yourself included), their actions, and what's influencing them for what they really are, and at that point, you can begin to war against the real enemy with lasting impact.

What lies has the enemy sold you and your family? What behaviors or beliefs have developed into puppet strings that have molded your reality (maybe for generations)? What things that you know are outside of the will of God for your life have you agreed with and allowed to survive or even thrive? Are you willing to continue living connected to those puppet strings? Are you content for those strings to grow until they destroy you or are transferred from you to your children or grandchildren one day?

Today's a new day, and what you do today will influence tomorrow. So what's it going to be? Freedom begins with changing your mind about whether or not these things are even acceptable, and then determining that they are not going to continue to thrive and grow.

Admit today that these things are not God's best for you and your future family. Determine that you are going to quit allowing them to so easily influence you, and instead choose to focus on and agree with God's desires for your life. Be the best you that you can be as you allow yourself to be guided and empowered by the Holy Spirit.

As we continue on, we will address the authority that you have as a child of God to directly address these strongholds in your life and family. And we will begin to cut some strings.

Chapter 23

Suit Up for Battle

I can remember the words "Suit up!" screamed out by the lieutenant when the emergency SWAT call would come in. In that moment, all of us would strip off our normal work clothes (as a detective, for me that was a suit and tie), and we would pull out the black BDU pants and shirts, knee pads, steel-toed combat boots, bullet-proof vests with one-inch-thick ceramic plates designed to protect us from high-velocity rounds, special belts to carry our additional equipment (pepper spray, extra magazines and bullets, and side arm), Kevlar helmets, gas masks, MP5 submachine guns, and AR-15s.

We trained as a unit; we dressed as a unit; we operated as a unit. Each one of us was fully equipped to address, combat, and, if necessary, eliminate the threat. The department made sure we had the best equipment necessary to preserve our lives and defend the lives of those we were being sent out to protect, and each piece of that equipment was meant to function for a specific purpose to allow us to function, contribute, and win as a team and defeat our enemy.

Put on All of God's Armor

In the previous chapter we discussed what the Bible addresses in Ephesians 6:12 regarding who our enemy really is. If you read verses 11–18 in that chapter you will see that when facing that enemy, God has actually provided for us *spiritual armor* that will contribute to our success for the battles we face.

Put on all of God's armor so that you will be able to stand firm against all strategies of the devil.
(Ephesians 6:11 NLT)

The Bible says that you are to put all of the armor on. Each piece has a purpose when it comes to defeating a spiritual enemy, so that when you are in the midst of battle, you will be standing firm in opposition. And failing to include a piece of that armor leaves an area uncovered and vulnerable to attack.

Stand your ground, putting on the belt of truth and the body armor of God's righteousness. For shoes, put on the peace that comes from the Good News so that you will be fully prepared. In addition to all of these, hold up the shield of faith to stop the fiery arrows of the devil. Put on salvation as your helmet, and take the sword of the Spirit, which is the word of God. Pray in the Spirit at all times and on every occasion. Stay alert and be persistent in your prayers for all believers everywhere.
(Ephesians 6:14–18 NLT)

Breaking It Down

Verse 14 tells us to put on the belt of truth and the body armor of God's righteousness. We discussed in previous chapters the importance of seeing the truth of who you are in Christ and how you are righteous (in right standing and justified) in God's eyes. We see in verse 14 that this understanding actually becomes a weapon of defense against a deceitful enemy who would try to convince you to believe his lies.

Verse 15 says to put shoes of peace on your feet. Your feet are your foundation and that which all of what God has for you stands and advances upon. If you don't understand the truth of righteousness in verse 14, then you won't have the peace needed and found in verse 15 through the grace and love of God (the good news). And then in times of battle you will find yourself unprepared because your foundation is shaky.

Verse 16 says to grab the shield of faith that will directly protect you from the arrows sent to kill and destroy you by your enemy. As we have so frequently stated in previous chapters, what

Suit Up for Battle

you believe will dictate how you respond. You don't have to tell me what you believe because your actions show me.

In times of direct combat with your enemy, it is what you believe about the truth, righteousness (v. 14), and the peace that comes as a result (v. 15) that ultimately gives you the strength not to be touched or impacted by the arrows the enemy sends to destroy you. Are you seeing how what you *think* about influences what you ultimately *believe* and subsequently what you *receive*?

Verse 17 tells us that salvation (which is solidified by grace through faith according to Ephesians 2:8–9) is our helmet and protects our head (which ultimately decides what we will believe and controls the rest of our actions) and how the Word of God becomes our double-edged offensive and defensive weapon to cut and strike down our enemy.

Verse 18 says to take all of those instructions and then stay vigilant and pray to see the breakthrough take place. We must do this with intentionality. We need to remain aware that there is an enemy who still wants to take us out and who has a plan for our destruction when he lies to us and attempts to convince us to do or believe something that we know is not God's best for us. In those moments we should utilize the authority God has given us, equipped with His armor.

When we believe and exercise faith toward what and who God says He is (and what and who He says we are), we become equipped with the complete weaponry necessary to fight and defeat our spiritual enemy in whatever physical form his puppets take on. Then, covered by the armor of God, your prayers and declarations are infused with agreement and faith, and the mountains of opposition in your life begin to move.

In James 2:19, the Bible says that faith is not defined by just believing there is a God, because even the demons believe that there's a God. On the contrary, true faith, according to that chapter, is actually defined by what you do. In other words, your actions reveal what you really believe.

In Hebrews 11:6, the Bible also says of faith that without it, it's impossible to please God (or to completely agree with God). So it would seem that being intentional about placing our agreement with the Word of God is an essential aspect of extending and exhibiting faith when it comes to combating the principalities and powers that come to steal, kill, and destroy.

These scriptures seem to make it apparent that perhaps many of our spiritual defeats have been directly connected to what we did not know and as a result did not believe (or possibly wrongly believed and wrongly agreed with). And maybe this is why the Bible says in Hosea 4:6, "My people are destroyed from lack of knowledge" (the King James version also says "lack of vision" in Proverbs 29:18).

It's time for you to "suit up" and become equipped with God's armor and actually defeat your enemy, protected by and empowered with the weaponry He has provided for you! You can do it. God's got you covered from head to toe. After all, it is *His* armor.

Chapter 24

You Don't Have to Walk in Fear Anymore

In the previous sections and corresponding chapters, we've discussed who God is, who we are, and where we've been, and now we're learning how to process where we are. By this point, you are likely beginning to understand that the enemy has strategically instituted strongholds into your life in order to be able to control you and keep you from becoming who you were created to be. He's convinced believers around the world to believe a lie because he knows when your belief is in his lie, you empower him as the liar.

I have found that one of the key weapons the Devil attacks believers with is the stronghold of fear. I struggled significantly with this stronghold. As a child I was afraid of everything. I was afraid of the dark. I was afraid of bad things happening to my family. I was afraid that I was going to get some dreaded disease. I was afraid of confrontation. I was afraid of being in front of people. I would nervously shake when another student was yelled at by a teacher. Fear tormented me, and I was embarrassed of how fearful I was. Fear was a stronghold placed there by the Devil that was intended to keep me from reaching my full potential, and it has likely been (in some extent) for the same reason strategically placed in your life as well.

My sister is two years younger than I am, and I can remember being ten or eleven years old, going to the amusement park, and crying because I was terrified to ride the roller coaster that she was excited to ride. Another time, in the sixth grade, I was confronted by a student who threatened to beat me up in the hallway. I can still remember the feeling of sitting in class, shaking and crying and being terribly embarrassed as the other students stared at me.

I hated being afraid because it made me feel weak. So as a teenager I decided to do the things I was afraid of until I wasn't afraid to do them anymore. I rode the roller coasters. I turned off the lights. I joined the drama club and got up in front of people. I volunteered to preach for youth night at our church. And eventually I got past being controlled by fear. It wasn't that I never felt fear; it wasn't that fear didn't ever try to attach itself to some other event or thought in my life. I was just determined not to allow it to manipulate my decisions anymore.

Fear Is the Root

Fear is so often the root of many other strongholds. For example, because you fear what others think, maybe your self-esteem becomes wounded and insecurity sets in. From the point of insecurity, many coping mechanisms (like alcohol abuse, drug use, and emotional eating) or protection mechanisms (like emotional walls, control issues, or even unhealthy attachments to others) set in. From those places, any number of dysfunctional behavioral patterns can develop in order to fill the void created, all from the root of fear being established first.

Fear is actually an indicator that what you believe at a heart level is not in complete agreement with the Word of God. Your enemy uses fear against you to destroy you, and it is probably the number one enemy of faith in God because it's difficult (if not impossible) to walk in faith and agreement with God's Word while living in fear.

The fear we feel is many times a byproduct of a belief (or faith) that we have in something other than the Word of God. For example, if God says you are loved, favored by Him, and called according to His purposes, but you constantly feel a need to appear to be better, to impress and be accepted by people, or are concerned about making it in life, then there's likely a good chance that you believe more in the lie that the Devil is selling you than the truth of who God says you are.

You Don't Have to Walk in Fear Anymore

The Bible says that King David was a man after God's own heart (1 Samuel 13:14; Acts 13:22). David abused his authority, committed adultery, and then had the husband of the woman he slept with killed. In ways likely more intense than most of our issues, David messed up. If we were labeling him by his sin, he could wear several scarlet letters. But his example should give us hope because God used David and embrace him when he turned his heart back to God. Even though he sinned, God was willing to define him as *a man after God's own heart*.

David had a faith in God that set him apart from others, and I believe it was because of his faith that he was able to accomplish so much and is revered as the greatest king in Israel's history. The way King David, a man who faced many dangerous battles, looked at life and circumstances is made clear by his own words in Psalm 27.

> *The LORD is my light and my salvation; whom shall I fear?*
> *The LORD is the strength of my life; of whom shall I be afraid?*
> (v. 1 KJV)

It's not likely that David didn't ever *feel* fear. As a matter of fact, some of the psalms he wrote indicated that he did, but then he would encourage himself with words that affirmed and focused on who he knew God to be, in spite of the circumstances.

F.E.A.R.: Face Everything and Rise

I recently heard a pastor say that fear can be an acronym for two things:

> *Forget Everything and Run*
> or
> *Face Everything and Rise*

Focus can fuel fear, or focus can fuel faith. Because David was aware of who God was in his life, he focused on the Lord's presence and he did not walk in fear. When he heard the giant Goliath, who struck fear in the hearts of an entire nation of warriors, mock and challenge the Lord's chosen people, he asked,

"Who does this Philistine who has no covenant with God think he is to come against the people of God?"

Satan used Goliath to cause fear by taunting the children of Israel and attempting to keep them from the victory that was theirs by inheritance because they were in covenant with God—until a warrior who knew his God and knew who he was as a child of God stood up in faith against him. And he will use something or someone to come after you too, and just like David, you can stand up and fight, and be victorious!

The Devil has a purpose for attacking you with fear. He has placed it there to keep you from your destiny and to create a ceiling for your progress. He knows that if he can get you to believe a lie before you equip yourself with the armor of God and step out in faith, then he is empowered to steal from you the very thing God has prepared for you!

God has not given you a spirit of fear. Fear is not a fruit produced of His Spirit. As a matter of fact, the Bible instructs you, "Let not your heart be troubled" (John 14:1 KJV) and "Do not be afraid" (v. 27). It's written as if it's a choice—because it is.

Fear not, for I am with you;
Be not dismayed, for I am your God.
I will strengthen you,
Yes, I will help you,
I will uphold you with My righteous right hand.
(Isaiah 41:10 NKJV)

The Bible says that "perfect love drives out all fear" (1 John 4:18). There is no more perfect love than the love that God has for you. Cast your cares upon Him, and give Him the areas that you have built walls around to protect yourself. You can trust Him with your heart. God is faithful.

Direct your focus like David did on who God is in your life. See yourself being empowered by the Holy Spirit of the God who created the universe! Let that focus fuel your faith to be more than you have ever been, and begin taking steps to becoming all that God has created you to be.

You don't have to walk in fear anymore.

Chapter 25

Fruit Is a Byproduct

Fruit is an organic byproduct of the tree that produces it. A healthy orange tree, planted in the proper soil and the proper environment receiving the proper nutrition of sunlight and water, if not infested with bugs, parasites, or disease that would steal the nutrition or devour the fruit, will organically produce healthy, good fruit effortlessly!

But in order to have a healthy orange harvest, there's a natural process that needs to be followed. Take that tree out of a Florida orange grove and place it in a Michigan apple orchard and that tree will remain barren. The apple trees around it will flourish and produce huge, shiny, red apples, but that orange tree will shrivel up and die. The answer to why is a simple one. The tree has to be planted in the environment it was created to flourish in, or the fruit will be compromised.

As a pastor who has been in ministry for over twenty years, I have found after speaking with a great many people that when they peel back the layers of their life, they are actually looking for one of three things (or maybe some combination of them) and doing whatever they feel is necessary to get them. Those three things are love, joy, and peace.

When they don't find love and joy, they find temporary peace at the bottom of a bottle. When they don't have peace, they compensate with an attempt at love in a new relationship or in the affirmation of someone who makes them feel good. It becomes a vicious cycle because not having one usually costs or spirals into the inability to experience the others.

It's not that the fruits of the Spirit are not attainable. I believe that we as human beings were created to experience them. The problem lies in the pursuit of these fruits in orchards where they cannot be naturally produced.

The Bible says this about the fruit that is produced in the life of a believer when the Holy Spirit resides within him:

> *But the fruit of the Spirit [the result of His presence within us] is love [unselfish concern for others], joy, [inner] peace, patience [not the ability to wait, but how we act while waiting], kindness, goodness, faithfulness, gentleness, self-control.*
> *Against such things there is no law.*
> (Galatians 5:22–23 AMP)

I believe that man was always intended to experience, walk in, and produce the fruit of the Holy Spirit in his life because he was created to have a personal and intimate relationship with God. He was always intended to be sustained by that relationship. The first three fruits listed are also the top three things people feel like they are missing when they are not in an intimate relationship with God.

Although the first step to experiencing these fruits is connection with God, many believers who love God still find themselves struggling to see these fruits produced in their lives. Then the question naturally becomes, *Why am I struggling?*

You don't see an orange tree straining to produce fruit like it's having to push it out of its branches. Yet this is the experience many believers describe as it pertains to producing the fruits of the Spirit. In these circumstances, there are two likely candidates keeping the fruit from producing.

The first is nutrition. Without sunlight and water, no plant can produce the fruit it was created to produce. Believers who find themselves struggling to produce fruit that should be effortlessly manifesting through their relationship with God need to ask themselves, *Am I feeding myself spirit-healthy food?*

Are you only filling your mind and spirit with junk (spending time watching, listening to, and reading stuff that doesn't contribute to your spiritual growth) and neglecting the

Fruit Is a Byproduct

essential nutrition found in intentionally spending time with God in prayer and spiritual development? Are you reading the Bible? Are you reading any books that challenge you to experience a deeper understanding of God and His Word? Are you attending a church or listening to any teachings that would help your spirit grow stronger? Or are you starving your spirit and not experiencing the fruit of a balanced relationship with God?

The second factor that may be influencing spiritual-fruit development in your life and robbing you of the love, joy, and peace that God says is yours is from what I would consider bugs, parasites, and disease. These are external factors often revealed as the strongholds that we have discussed throughout the course of this book (fears, insecurities, addictions, unhealthy habitual choices, negative thought patterns, etc., tied to events in life that have limited your spiritual growth). They have over time infiltrated your experience in such a way that you have simply learned to tolerate them and live with the discomfort of them, and have become resolved to complacency as it pertains to living satisfied with inadequate fruit production.

You will know them by their fruits. Do men gather grapes from thorn bushes or figs from thistles? Even so, every good tree bears good fruit, but a bad tree bears bad fruit. A good tree cannot bear bad fruit, nor can a bad tree bear good fruit. . . .
Therefore by their fruits you will know them.
(Matthew 7:16–20 NKJV)

Verse 20 above is not a matter of judgment of good and bad as much as it is a matter of simple observation. When you were made alive in Christ, all things became new. Not only are you intended to experience the fruits of the Spirit, experiencing them is not supposed to be hard or strenuous. If it is, then the fruit production should be an indicator that something is out of alignment and needs to be addressed in order for there to be a resolve.

You are who God says you are. His promises are intended to be fulfilled in your life. The fruits of the Spirit are a part of your inheritance as a believer, and the first step to experiencing them in your daily life is reaching a place of understanding and believing that you are supposed to experience them.

You were created for more! You can and you will experience more as the knowledge you are obtaining by reading this book is opening the doors for the limitless freedom and potential you were created to walk in.

Chapter 26

What Happens in the Mind Will Happen in Time

My son comes to me nearly daily saying, "Daddy, I had this weird thought today . . ." He's definitely my kid. I can say with all assurance that if people knew some of the bizarre stuff that jumps into my head, they'd probably at times question my sanity. Sometimes I have to laugh at how ridiculous my thoughts can be.

It's not a sin to have an ungodly or faithless thought. The Devil will make sure he plants *tons* of those into your imagination, in hopes that you will meditate on them. The sin is not in the initial thought; the sin is in what you do with it.

When I teach my Experiencing Freedom classes, I often share this example. It's not a sin for a guy to see a girl rollerblading down the boardwalk and think, *Wow, she's pretty!* But if he goes back around the block to get a more detailed look at what curves he might have missed the first time, he's standing on the edge of a slippery slope.

As a believer seeking to please God, I can say with all confidence that the Devil will do what he can to get you to think about and meditate on whatever unhealthy thoughts he can get you to give attention to. For some it will be thoughts of worthlessness; for others it will be lustful imaginations; for others it will be contemplating the violence you will respond with if that person ever does "that thing" to you again.

These are unhealthy thoughts designed to get you to imagine, meditate on, and be distracted by that which is contrary to the Word of God. The Devil knows that *what happens in the mind will happen in time*, and the more you actually place yourself in a scenario in your mind, the more likely you are to respond in the way that you imagined.

Nobody goes to school one day and accidentally cheats on their test or goes to a party and accidentally gets drunk. If you train your body and mind beforehand to do what you have repeatedly imagined, when the time comes, very little thought is needed to convince you to engage in the negative action or mentality that the enemy has been grooming your imaginations with.

Many times faith and unbelief are cultivated the same way. For the person who fixes their minds on the things of God, when difficulties and opposition come, they resort to the faith they have built up in their private prayers, thoughts, and studies.

But the person who meditates on negative, faithless, unbelieving thoughts has trained his mind toward the power of evil and the expectation of bad things instead of the power and promises of God. Then, when the opposition actually comes, unbelief is what he is left to stand upon, and he finds himself often defeated before the battle even begins. His lack of intentionality toward exercising and implementing faith has made it impossible to fully agree with God when it becomes necessary to do so.

Casting Down Imaginations

As we see in the scripture below, when thoughts come that are not in alignment with God's Word, we are instructed to be intentional in casting them down by renouncing them with our mouths and declaring the truth that the lie would attempt to sell us. We bring them into submission by refusing to dwell on thoughts that contradict the Word of God over our lives.

For though we walk in the flesh, we do not war according to the flesh. For the weapons of our warfare are not carnal but mighty in God for pulling down strongholds, casting down arguments (imaginations) and every high thing that exalts itself against the knowledge of God, bringing every thought into captivity to the obedience of Christ.
(2 Corinthians 10:3–5 NKJV)

What Happens in the Mind Will Happen in Time

Although the initial catalyst that created the stronghold may have been spiritual, strongholds live and grow in the soul (mind, will, and emotions) influenced by what we believe and place our agreement in. This is why casting down imaginations and everything that exalts itself against the knowledge of God and bringing every thought into captivity to the obedience of Christ are so essential. After all, as a man thinks in his heart, so is he . . . right?

It is absolutely imperative that we do not develop a passive theology, mind-set, or belief system that accommodates or excuses thoughts that lead us down the path of faithlessness or unbelief. If God says that we are overcomers (1 John 5:4–5) or more than conquerors (Romans 8:31–39) or that we can do all things through Christ who strengthens us (Philippians 4:13) or that we are loved by Him (1 John 4:10–19), we cannot allow, meditate upon, or excuse thoughts that contradict those words of God that are ultimately our weapons against the lies of the enemy!

If God is for us, who can be against us? . . . Who shall bring a charge against God's elect? It is God who justifies. Who is he who condemns? . . . We are more than conquerors through Him who loved us.
(Romans 8:31, 33–34, 37 NKJV)

The Devil will make sure these negative thoughts come when you are talking to God, or praying for someone else, or dreaming about being the person God created you to be. Some of you have probably even had some very off-the-wall thoughts bombard your mind while reading this book. Why do you think that is? It's because the Devil knows if he can distract you from the truth, then you won't live in the fullness of it.

James 4:7 says to "submit yourself, then, to God. Resist the devil, and he will flee." Deuteronomy 28:7 says, "The LORD will cause the enemies who rise up against you to be defeated before you; they will come out against you one way, but flee before you seven ways" (AMP). And Isaiah 59:19 reads, "When the enemy comes in like a flood, the Spirit of the LORD will lift up a standard against him" (NKJV). When those faithless, unbelieving thoughts come in, the way we cast down those thoughts and bring them into captivity is to contradict the lie being sold to us with what the Word of God says (which is exactly what Jesus did when He was tempted by the Devil in Matthew 4 and Luke 4).

And do not be conformed to this world, but be transformed by the renewing of your mind, that you may prove what is that good and acceptable and perfect will of God.
(Romans 12:2 NKJV)

The Bible says in Romans 12:2, "Be transformed by the renewing of your mind." We can completely transform our lives, live beyond the temptation of sin, and overcome all the attacks of the enemy by intentionally meditating on God's words and thoughts toward us, and subsequently renewing (reprograming) our thoughts with His thoughts.

We discussed earlier that the sword of the Spirit is the Word of God. Psalm 119:11 states, "Your word I have hidden in my heart, that I might not sin against You" (NKJV), and Romans 10:8 says the word of faith is in your heart and in your mouth. When the enemy attacks your mind with the lie, you need to speak and declare like Jesus did the truth of the Word of God out loud.[4]

When the Devil tells you that you can't, say out loud, "I can do all things through Christ who gives me strength."

When he says you are a failure, say, "I'm more than a conqueror through God who loves me!"

When he tells you God is mad at you or that you are unworthy, say, "I am the righteousness of God in Christ, I am His child, and I am loved by Him!"

You can't always control the thoughts that come in, but you can control what you do with them. You can choose to cast them down, submit them to God's authority, and rob those negative thoughts of their power. What you choose to meditate on, you give life to.

---

[4] For some additional examples declarations and confessions visit my website www.LimitlessSolutions.org.

Satan Is Not the Opposite of God

According to Romans 16:20 and Luke 10:19, God crushes Satan under the feet of the empowered believer. Contrary to common belief, the Devil is not the *opposite* of God. As a fallen archangel, he's maybe the opposite of Michael or Gabriel, but he's nowhere near the scale and caliber of the God of the universe whose Holy Spirit resides within you and fills you with limitless authority, power, and potential over all the works of the Devil.

What you tolerate, you authorize to exist. You've been given the power to place a demand on your freedom and the enemy who tries to steal it from you. Matthew 18:18 says, "Whatever you bind on earth will be bound in heaven, and whatever you loose on earth will be loosed in heaven." Many believers are waiting on God to do for them what He has empowered them to do for themselves.

Draw a line in the sand today. Determine now what you will do the next time the enemy attempts to influence your meditations with ungodly thoughts. Actions reveal nature, and pursuit is proof of desire. If you truly do desire to operate to the fullest degree of your potential and experience the limitless power and freedom over the enemy of your soul, then implement today the practices that you want to be established tomorrow. What you do daily, you become permanently.

Chapter 27

Forgive and Forget?

Overcoming unforgiveness is an absolutely essential aspect of getting from where you *are* to where you are *going*. But what it actually means may be much different from what you have been taught. As I stated in chapter 18 (but it bears repeating for this example), the person who coined the phrase, "When life deals you lemons, make lemonade," has likely never been dealt a rotten lemon.

In my studies I came across a quote from a very well-respected man in freedom ministry circles on the topic of unforgiveness. He stated (and I will paraphrase his statement): If you cannot restore the relationship that was wounded in the offense to the place it was before the offense, then you have not completely forgiven the person who has offended you.

I personally feel like that kind of a broad statement is irresponsible if not prefaced with clearly defined circumstances where it can be applied. Kind of like the "make lemonade" statement, there are some circumstances that simply do not fit inside of the boundaries of his perspective.

If we are talking about a former friend talking trash about me, or my youth pastor saying something during youth group that I thought was directed toward me, or a family member wronging me by doing something that hurt my feelings . . . then yes, I agree that circumstances like these where we have been offended probably fit within the box of this perspective. It's true that we probably get more emotionally involved in stupid and trivial issues that we will likely not even care about by this time next year. And when dealing with the "dumb stuff" we should look to restore the relationship to where it was before, if at all possible. Life is too short to allow the little things to have such a big impact on our lives.

However, if a family member molested my child, it would be the opposite of using wisdom to place my child around that family member again. In that situation, it would cause more damage to the child to further subject them to their offender. So it wouldn't mean that I was walking in unforgiveness not to allow the relationship to be restored to its previous place. It would mean that I was using discernment.

*So now there is no condemnation
for those who belong to Christ Jesus.*
(Romans 8:1 NLT)

Many people don't really know what it means to forgive. We are told to forgive and forget but fail to recognize that *forgetting* is not a human characteristic. The Bible says that God forgets our sins, and somewhere along the line we have decided that this is what we are to do as well. Then we feel like we are not forgiving the way God would have us do, and feelings of condemnation set in (which we have already discussed in earlier chapters are not from God). But understand this: because we remember or because it still hurts does not mean we have not forgiven; it means we are human.

Over years of ministry I've had so many people come to me in brokenness because they read scriptures like Matthew 6:15 or Mark 11:26 that say if you do not forgive others then God cannot forgive you. They interpret this to mean that because they still have difficulty when they remember what happened to them that they are walking in unforgiveness, and subsequently, God can't forgive them.

When taking these scriptures in proper context, the Bible is speaking of recognizing our own failures in life and the fact that God has freely forgiven us for everything we have done. Because we too have messed up and been forgiven of much by God, we should not place ourselves in positions of self-righteousness by viewing ourselves as better than others or holding sin against them.

Extending forgiveness does not have some trust prerequisite or mandate attached to it. The person you are forgiving does not have to be trusted because you have forgiven them. Even 2 Corinthians 8 and 1 Timothy 3 outline that the character of believers should be tested for greed or dishonest gain before being trusted. If they failed the test, forgiveness could be extended, but that does not mean that their overseers should place them in charge of the treasury department. That would be foolishness that would set them both up for unnecessary difficulty.

Forgiveness Is Not a Feeling, but a Choice!

Because we are so feelings-oriented and likely because of what we have been taught regarding what forgiveness looks like, many struggle with the fear that because they still feel a certain way about a situation they are walking in unforgiveness. While our feelings may be an indicator of unforgiveness, they are not the absolute indicator. Because forgiveness is not a feeling. Forgiveness is a choice!

When those young men tried to kill me years ago, ending my career as a law enforcement officer and to date costing me a million dollars in lost wages (between my career and the personal business I had to sell), I chose that day to forgive them.

How? Why?

The forgiveness was not so much about them as it was about me. It was about guarding my heart and recognizing the impact that unforgiveness can have on my outcomes in life. When I was in the hospital hours after they attacked me (and while one of the young men was in a room two doors down being guarded by officers from another county for his own safety), I told my coworkers (who were furious that these guys attacked me) that I chose to forgive them. It wasn't about a feeling; it was about a choice, and I chose to do what I knew was right—even though I was severely wounded. This is what Christ modeled on the cross when He cried out to God, "Father, forgive them, for they do not know what they are doing" (Luke 23:34).

Forgive and Forget?

In my case, although I made the initial decision to forgive, it wasn't a one-and-done kind of situation. Over the course of the next year when I was in physical rehab for sometimes five to six hours a day, or on a psychiatrist's couch trying to get over the PTSD, or taking emotion-suppressing drugs to get past the panic attacks, let's just say I had *many* opportunities to choose to forgive them again. I made the same choice again and again.

Everybody's circumstances are different, and in my own experiences, I feel it's easier to forgive someone of something that happens to me personally than it is to extend forgiveness to someone who has hurt someone I love. My wife didn't understand why two days after I was attacked, I was purchasing Bibles to give to these guys. She wasn't quite there yet.

Forgiveness Begins Where You Are

Regardless of when you are able to extend forgiveness, it's vital to realize that sometimes forgiveness is from week to week, sometimes it is day to day, sometimes it is hour to hour, and sometimes it is minute to minute! Forgiveness is choosing to let the person and the offense go and not allowing them to occupy the mental real estate that will plague your progress. Lewis B. Smedes said it this way in his book *Forgive and Forget: Healing the Hurts We Don't Deserve*: "To forgive is to set a prisoner free and discover that the prisoner was you."

Think about how much life you have missed out on because you did not let go of an offense. Holding on to the offense and allowing it to continue to victimize you is not hurting the person who wronged you . . . it's hurting you!

Choosing to forgive is as simple as saying, "I refuse to allow them to hurt me anymore. I refuse to allow my emotions to be influenced by offense. I refuse to hold this to their account. I leave justice in the hands of God, and I release them. I choose to forgive them and let them go."

So the next time you remember the offense (and you will), release them again (even if it's only five minutes later). Initially, this will likely be more frequent (especially if you have spent a lot of time in unforgiveness), but in time you will reprogram your habits, and choosing forgiveness again will be the default response instead of the negative bitterness that has stolen your peace.

Chapter 28

Four Hundred Ninety

In Matthew 18, Peter comes to Jesus and asks him, "Lord, how many times shall I forgive my brother or sister who sins against me? Up to seven times?" (v. 21). Jesus' response blows Peter away when he tells him that he should forgive him "seventy times seven" (v. 22 NLT), or in other words, 490 times!

So should you keep a list of how many times you've forgiven a person? No. The number could as well have been a million. What Jesus was saying is you should forgive *every time.* In another scripture Jesus says that if you bring your offering to the church and then you remember that someone has something against you, you should straighten that out first and then give your offering to God (Matthew 5:23–24). So why is it so important to God that we not carry offense or harbor unforgiveness? Because it has a significant ability to choke out the blessings that God has for you.

We spoke in previous chapters about reaping and sowing. After years of ministering to people and having them experience freedom from strongholds in their lives, I'm convinced that unforgiveness is one of the most significant barriers to experiencing breakthrough and blessings.

When we live with unforgiveness, it is like allowing a very aggressive weed to live in your garden. When Jesus instructs us not to even bring our offering to the church until the issue is resolved, I believe it is because unforgiveness has the power to choke out the harvest in the seed we are planting before it ever takes root.

The influence that unforgiveness has upon you soul (your mind, will, and emotions) is difficult to quantify, but if you have ever held bitterness and unforgiveness in your heart toward someone, you know the types of ungodly, negative, vindictive, and hurtful thoughts that accompany it, not to mention how it impacts mood changes, depression, anger, even physical sickness as your stomach gets in knots the longer you dwell on the offense. I believe that what happens in the mind will happen in time, and if this is true, our thoughts dictate what we end up experiencing, and then it's not difficult to imagine the far-reaching effects that refusing to forgive can have on our lives.

When you choose to forgive someone, you are not saying that what they did was not wrong. It is not expressing that you condone it. *You were wronged!* But as we said in the previous chapter, when you choose to forgive, you choose to refuse to hold on to the offense and allow it to continue to have a negative impact on you. Forgiveness is for your peace of mind!

When You Need to Forgive Yourself

Sometimes the most difficult person to forgive is you. Unforgiveness toward yourself is often identifiable by the guilt you carry about your past. If you were talking to a friend who experienced what you did, you would tell them a dozen reasons why their life is different now, that God has forgiven them, and that they need to allow themselves to be human. Yet, for whatever reason, it's a lot more difficult to give yourself the same grace that you would tell someone else to give themselves.

Whether directed toward someone else or directed toward yourself, unforgiveness has the same capacity to keep you from what God has for you. And it is resolved the same way.

Just like we addressed in the previous chapter, when you choose to forgive (yourself or anyone else) you choose to release the offense. If you are having difficulty forgiving yourself, every time you feel the guilt or have the negative thoughts, you need to say to yourself, "I've been forgiven by God, and I choose to receive that forgiveness and also forgive myself."

Ultimately forgiveness is the action of letting go. When walking people through forgiving someone, I will often instruct

Four Hundred Ninety

them to speak the name of the one who offended them into a closed fist, then to place their fists out in front of them and open their hand. This visual act impresses the importance of not holding on to something that only they can release.

Initially you may have to release them (or yourself) very frequently, but in time your feelings and emotions will begin to line up with your words and actions, and you will find yourself walking in a state of releasing the offense more frequently than a state of holding on to it.

Jesus has covered and forgiven *every sin you have ever committed*. It's important to allow yourself to extend your faith and come into agreement with what and who God's Word says you are, and not the image your past might paint of you. You are a new creation!

By this point it should be obvious why your enemy would like for you to remain bound by unforgiveness. As long as the weeds of unforgiveness are still alive and at work in your life, the blessings and open doors that God has for you remain out of reach for you. In essence, unforgiveness can choke out your progress and create a barrier that blocks the flow of blessing into your life.

Unforgiveness creates an environment for strife, bitterness, anger, and hatred to grow and produce fruit. The Bible says that this is the environment where every other evil work abounds (James 3:16).

Whether it's someone else or yourself, be intentional today to ask God to give you the strength to forgive and then make the decision not to hold on to the offense any longer. You don't need that stuff stealing from you anymore. It's time to choose to forgive and quit allowing your past to keep you today from where you are going tomorrow.

Part V

Where Am I Going?

God has a plan for your life. You were created to win and to be an ambassador of His kingdom! He has provided you with everything you need in order to combat your enemy and entirely experience His limitless freedom, power, and potential over strongholds and all the works of the enemy. But having a vision for where you are going and who you are in that process is essential.

Part V of this book will give you a more precise vision for what it means to implement all of what we have discussed in the previous four parts of this book. Where you are going is greater than any place you have ever been. The rest of your life will be the best of your life.

Winning is no longer a distant goal! Winning is a daily reality!

Chapter 29

Teach Us to Pray

Over the course of more than two decades in ministry, I've frequently been confronted with people (especially newer believers) who are actually intimidated to pray. They ask me questions like, "Pastor Aaron, how do I pray effectively?" and "What if my prayers don't sound like the pastor's?" They are worried that God doesn't hear the prayer if it doesn't sound professional.

But here's the secret—*there's no secret*. I talk to God just like I'd talk to you. Sometimes I talk a lot. Sometimes I just share a single thought and listen to see if He speaks anything to my spirit. Sometimes I don't say anything at all, but I know that my tears speak volumes about what I'm going through as I just sit there and focus on Him. I don't talk to God in the King's English (like the King James Bible) or pretend to be something I'm not. I don't say *thee*, *thou*, or any other word I wouldn't use in casual conversation. And you don't have to either.

It's important to understand that God created you the way He did on purpose. You are a unique individual and He made you that way. He doesn't expect you to look, act, or talk like someone you are not. You are unique because He made you that way, and He has no expectation that you should pretend to be someone you are not when you are approaching Him.

If you are angry, tell Him you are angry.

If you are hurt, tell Him you are hurt.

If you are thankful, thank Him.

And if you are afraid, let Him know that too. He can handle it!

Cast Your Cares on Him

You are not the first person in the world to ever feel or experience what you are experiencing, and you won't be the last. The Bible says that God wants you to cast your cares upon Him because He cares for you (1 Peter 5:7).

In the Bible, the disciples also struggled with understanding prayer as a formality. Jews (which all the disciples were) had a very highly religious, ritualistic, and formal approach to God. So when Jesus came along and contradicted many of the ideals that people had about who God was and how He felt about them (based upon what they had been taught), it left them with some legitimate questions.

In Matthew 6, Jesus responded to the disciple's request for Jesus to teach them how to pray with the following prayer:

> *Pray, then, in this way:*
> *"Our Father who is in heaven,*
> *Hallowed be Your name.*
> *Your kingdom come,*
> *Your will be done*
> *On earth as it is in heaven.*
> *Give us this day our daily bread.*
> *And forgive us our debts, as we have forgiven our debtors [letting go of both the wrong and the resentment].*
> *And do not lead us into temptation, but deliver us from evil. [For Yours is the kingdom and the power and the glory forever. Amen.]"*
> (vv. 9–13 AMP)

Jesus modeled an outline of how to approach God. It was not intended to be the *exact* and *only words* spoken, but rather a format in which to approach Him.

- Verse 9: "Hallowed be Your name": *Hallowed* means holy, honored, and respected. In essence Jesus is saying, "Remember, you are approaching the Holy and all-powerful God of the universe. Enter into His presence with a heart of worship first."

- Verse 10: "Your kingdom come, Your will be done on earth as it is in heaven": Acknowledge that experiencing God's kingdom is of the utmost importance to you and God, and pray for that to take place with the understanding that the kingdom of God manifested on earth should look like it does in heaven as we place our agreement in His will and Word.
- Verse 11: "Give us this day our daily bread": Pray for what you need. Tell God that you need Him to intervene in your circumstances and ask for His assistance.
- Verse 12: "And forgive us our debts, as we have forgiven our debtors [letting go of both the wrong and the resentment]": Take this time to ask God to forgive you of the things that are weighing on your mind and heart and interfering with your feelings of intimacy with Him through sin consciousness. Then be intentional to forgive those who have hurt you so that unforgiveness doesn't continue to choke out the blessings that God has for you.
- Verse 13: "And do not lead us into temptation, but deliver us from evil. For Yours is the kingdom and the power and the glory forever. Amen": Acknowledge the essential importance of God leading you and ordering up your footsteps, and ask the Holy Spirit to guide, direct, and protect you from any plans or attacks of the enemy that are set out to steal, kill, and destroy you. For it's His eternal kingdom and power manifested in your life for His glory and to fulfill His desires for we His children whom He so loves!

As an example, this is what a short prayer according to this format might look like,

- Verse 9: *God, You are so awesome and I acknowledge that without You I am lost!*
- Verse 10*: I pray today that You will open doors in my life to implement and carry Your will and kingdom to those who may not know You and that I would be an instrument of Your grace and love so they can experience freedom*

from the kingdom of darkness ruling in their lives on a scale that only the kingdom of heaven can provide for them.
- Verse 11: *Lord, You know what I'm dealing with myself. You know my hurts. You know my pain. You know my needs. You know the desire of my heart. I ask You to intervene in those circumstances today with Your mighty power.*
- Verse 12: *Forgive me of the things that I have done that have not honored our relationship, and I choose now to forgive those who have also dishonored my relationship with them.*
- Verse 13: *Protect me and my family today from any attacks of the enemy. I acknowledge that it is only You and Your grace and love for me that empowers me to represent You, and I ask that Your glory be displayed through me in every place I go today. Amen.*

What is important is not so much the *words* you pray as much as your intentionality *to pray*. This format may help you address some important points as you do.

As you know, any relationship you have is built upon the foundation of communication. Prayer is our communication with God. Make a decision today to be intentional in talking to God. Don't worry what it sounds like. Just be you and He'll be fine with that. He's waiting.

Chapter 30

Believe That You Shall Receive

In the previous chapter we addressed the Lord's Prayer from Matthew 6. I did an extensive study on this passage a few years ago and discovered something very interesting. When interpreting it from the Greek text and comparing it to the Aramaic language that Jesus would have likely spoken, there is some additional insight to glean from as it pertains to God and His proximity to us.

In the opening words of the Lord's Prayer, Jesus says, "Our Father in heaven, hallowed be Your name." The original text fully interpreted adds, "My God, You are my supply and are as close as the air that I am breathing. I stop now and become aware of You."

The power of those words gives me chills. God is as close to you as the air you are breathing. He's not somewhere in a distant galaxy watching us with some all-seeing telescope; He is with you and in direct proximity to you all the time! When you pray, you aren't praying to a God far off at the other end of the universe; you are talking to the God who is sitting next to you on the bed or standing next to you in the hallway.

You don't have to yell to get His attention. He hears the silent whisper and sees the pain in your eyes. You don't serve a God who is untouchable or distantly removed from you. On the contrary, the only thing that becomes a separation between you and God is your ability to see Him with your physical eyes.

Surrounded by God

The truth is you are surrounded by Him. Like the air you breathe, you are immersed in Him, and when you intentionally become aware of Him and communicate with Him, His words become alive and resonate within your spirit.

For me, understanding this personal proximity of the loving God of the universe did something extraordinary to encourage my faith. I find myself amazed by the fact that He is intricately involved with me. The Bible says He is so involved with us that He numbers the hairs on our head (Matthew 10:30)!

Now when I read scriptures that say He will never leave me or forsake me (Deuteronomy 31:6) or that He is a friend who sticks closer than a brother (Proverbs 18:24), I can visualize something so much more intimate and personal. He's not a God I will only experience somewhere in the future in heaven; He's with me right now. And He's looking over your shoulder right now as you are reading this book.

When He says He hears and answers your prayers, He's not doing it from light years away. From this perspective, the following scriptures come alive in ways that are so much more real and tangible.

I assure you and most solemnly say to you, whoever says to this mountain, "Be lifted up and thrown into the sea!" and does not doubt in his heart [in God's unlimited power], but believes that what he says is going to take place, it will be done for him [in accordance with God's will]. For this reason I am telling you, whatever things you ask for in prayer [in accordance with God's will], believe [with confident trust] that you have received them, and they will be given to you.
(Mark 11:23–24 AMP)

Keep on asking, and you will receive what you ask for. Keep on seeking, and you will find. Keep on knocking, and the door will be opened to you.
(Matthew 7:7 NLT)

You can pray for anything, and if you have faith, you will receive it.

Believe That You Shall Receive

(Matthew 21:22 NLT)

You can ask for anything in my name, and I will do it, so that the Son can bring glory to the Father.
Yes, ask me for anything in my name, and I will do it!
(John 14:13–14 NLT)

Are any of you sick? You should call for the elders of the church to come and pray over you, anointing you with oil in the name of the Lord. Such a prayer offered in faith will heal the sick, and the Lord will make you well. And if you have committed any sins, you will be forgiven. Confess your sins to each other and pray for each other so that you may be healed. The earnest prayer of a righteous person has great power and produces wonderful results.
(James 5:14–16 NLT)

Don't worry about anything; instead, pray about everything. Tell God what you need, and thank him for all he has done. Then you will experience God's peace, which exceeds anything we can understand. His peace will guard your hearts and minds as you live in Christ Jesus.
(Philippians 4:6–7 NLT)

My hope is that this revelation of God's proximity to you ignites greater levels of faith than you have ever experienced. It did for me. God's inspired Word is His expressed will for you. His promises are for you to experience today.

For no matter how many promises God has made, they are "Yes" in Christ. And so through him the "Amen" is spoken by us to the glory of God.
(2 Corinthians 1:20)

I become overwhelmed with excitement reading 2 Corinthians 1:20 in the New International Version when it says, "The 'Amen' is spoken by us to the glory of God." In essence it's saying, we place *our agreement* in the promises of God when we say, "Amen [so be it]," and the faith that is released in our agreement with His Word (promises) brings glory to God as those promises are manifested and made alive in our lives.

God is so good. He loves you so much. He wants you to experience so much more than you may have ever even known was possible. And as you become more and more aware of the freedom He has provided, the bondage of yesterday is abolished and the chains are broken off of tomorrow.

Chapter 31

Kingdom Authority

With the billions upon billions of planets in our universe, God could have certainly chosen to send Satan anywhere after casting him out of heaven. I think it's safe to say we can all agree that he belongs in hell. But he isn't there yet. God chose to send Satan to this earth, the same place He made for us, and then gave us dominion over it (and Satan).

In Genesis 1:27–30, God created man and then gave him authority over the earth. In Psalm 115:16, the Bible says that the heavens are the Lord's but the earth He has given to mankind. God always intended to use mankind to rule the earth and establish God's kingdom through the authority He gave us, and I'm convinced that a part of that involved ruling over Satan as God's representatives on the earth. But the choice of whether or not we ever utilized that authority was always up to us.

When Adam chose to sin instead of follow the instruction of God, he submitted his authority to the rule and institution of another kingdom, the kingdom of sin, and that kingdom had its own reaping and sowing principles (the most significant being death).

That Which Was Lost

Most Bible scholars agree that Jesus' primary message was the kingdom of God. Even when He taught His disciples to pray in Matthew 6, Jesus referenced the kingdom of God being established on earth "as it is in heaven" (v. 10). I believe God always intended for us, His children, created in His likeness, to institute the rule and culture of heaven here on the earth just like Jesus did.

Matthew 18:11 says that Jesus came to save "that which was lost" (NASB). It doesn't say *those*; it says *that*. I believe the *that* which was lost was the authority that God gave man and man subsequently surrendered to the kingdom of sin. And of course, sin produced its own fruit on the earth, which ultimately kept us from fully seeing what God's way would look like if we had followed His leading from the beginning.

Now the practices of the sinful nature are clearly evident: they are sexual immorality, impurity, sensuality (total irresponsibility, lack of self-control), idolatry, sorcery, hostility, strife, jealousy, fits of anger, disputes, dissensions, factions [that promote heresies], envy, drunkenness, riotous behavior, and other things like these. I warn you beforehand, just as I did previously, that those who practice such things will not inherit the kingdom of God. But the fruit of the Spirit [the result of His presence within us] is love [unselfish concern for others], joy, [inner] peace, patience [not the ability to wait, but how we act while waiting], kindness, goodness, faithfulness, gentleness, self-control.
Against such things there is no law.
(Galatians 5:19–23 AMP)

Verse 21 says, "Those who practice such things [sin] will not inherit the kingdom of God." Many assume that this is talking about going to hell or missing heaven. But I wonder if possibly it might mean more than that. When I read this scripture, I don't see the repercussions as being somewhere *down the road* after death, but rather as immediate and instantaneous.

I believe that a Christian can get drunk, fall down, hit his head and die, and still go to heaven. I believe that you can be a Christian, experience varying levels of immorality, and still get to heaven. But what I don't believe is that you can do these things (which are rooted in the kingdom of darkness), have fruit that produces death and chokes out blessing springing up in your life, and at the same time operate unfazed by those fruits. I believe that the limitless potential you have been given by God can become limited when sinful choices go unaddressed and the fruits of those choices grow unopposed.

When Jesus restored that which was lost, He restored our authority and the ability to experience the benefits and promises associated with establishing God's kingdom on earth. We don't have to live bound by the Devil, because Christ purchased our freedom and restored our authority over the enemy!

But He was wounded for our transgressions, He was bruised for our iniquities; the chastisement for our peace was upon Him, and by His stripes we are healed.
(Isaiah 53:5 NKJV)

Experiencing salvation is more than just going to heaven. When Jesus died, He saved us from our sin, but He also saved us from the curses that accompanied sin in the world. In Isaiah 53:5 above, the Bible says that Jesus was wounded, bruised, crushed, and broken for our transgressions and iniquities (transgressions and iniquities are sinful behaviors), the punishment for us to have peace was placed upon Him, and by His stripes we are made healed.

At the same time Jesus purchased your freedom from sin, He purchased your peace and your healing. Salvation is all-inclusive. Everything that was lost when man surrendered his authority to the kingdom of sin was restored by Jesus on the cross, and He intended for us to experience the benefits of salvation in the earth as well as in eternity.

Do You Believe It?

The thing about authority is, you have to believe you possess it before you will exercise it. When people don't know that they are allowed to do something, they hesitate and wait for confirmation before they act. When they don't know if they *can* (or are allowed to), most of the time they *won't*.

Listen carefully: I have given you authority [that you now possess] to tread on serpents and scorpions, and [the ability to

exercise authority] over all the power of the enemy (Satan); and nothing will [in any way] harm you.
(Luke 10:19 AMP)

It's very important that you recognize and believe that you were not created to live bound by sin and a slave to the Devil. According to the Bible, you have been given authority by Christ over all the power of the enemy (Luke 10:19)!

The Bible says when you stand against the Devil in opposition, he will flee from you (James 4:7). You don't have to be a pastor or even an adult to have authority over the Devil. You can tell him to get out of your life and shut his mouth when he speaks lies to your mind. He doesn't have any more rights to your life than you give him. So stand your ground against him today and utilize the authority that God created you to walk in.

The Devil is not over your head; he is under your feet (Ephesians 1:22; 1 Corinthians 15:27; Hebrews 2:8; 1 John 14:27). Treat him like it.

Chapter 32

It's Already in You

Jesus didn't say that the kingdom of God was only to be experienced after we died. On the contrary, Jesus prayed that the kingdom would be established "on earth as it is in heaven." Our freedom and dominion are not intended to be only experienced after we die but while we live—just like it was with Jesus!

In Matthew 3:2, 10:7, and Mark 1:15, Jesus said that the kingdom of God is at hand. And Luke 17:20–21 says that the kingdom of God is in you! I'm convinced that the authority that Jesus exampled was an indicator of what we can experience when we enter the fullness of understanding regarding who God is and who we are intended to be when He is our Savior.

I simply cannot believe that bondage to sin and death are what God intended for us when He created man in His image and likeness and then gave us dominion over the earth. As a matter of fact, Jesus completely contradicted that mind-set in John 10:10 when He said, "I have come that you might have life and experience it to the full."

Like the mentality of so many students who endure their classes and are just glad when they make it to the next grade, a great many believers have the same type of an escapist mentality as it pertains to life on earth. In their minds, they have been convinced that they are supposed to live their eighty years (give or take) while enduring all the evil attacks Satan can throw at them with a distant hope of a reward at the end in heaven when Jesus will say, "Well done, my good and faithful servant. You took some amazing butt-kickings and lived a humble life of lack and defeat, so now enter into your reward." But heaven in eternity is only the icing on the cake. Jesus didn't die for us only so we could go to heaven. On the contrary, He purchased our freedom and gave us His authority so we could bring heaven to every place on this earth!

A Mirror Image
Jesus said, "Anyone who has seen me has seen the father" (John 14:9). He also said that He didn't do anything except what He saw or heard the Father do. He was telling people, "If you want to know how God feels about a situation or what His will is regarding it, look at how I handle these things and you will have seen a mirror image of My Father and His will."

Jesus didn't live in a way that excused or cowered to the attack of the Devil. And the few times we see Him get frustrated with believers in the Bible is when they fail to implement what He taught them to do and don't utilize their authority and faith as children of God.

What you tolerate you authorize to exist, and I can't think of a single event in the Bible where Jesus tolerated Satan's attack. In every instance He told the demons what to do. Can you hear Him saying it? "Come out! Get behind Me!"

God is certainly big enough to use anything and turn it around for the good, but think about this—Jesus never blessed any storms.

He never told anyone who was suffering, "This is just the will of God to teach you a lesson and draw you closer to Him."

He never excused a disease or death with an explanation of "that person has to stay sick or die so that others will come to God through the tragedy."

On the contrary, Jesus brought the kingdom of God to every biblical occurrence of bondage, disease, lack, and even death and transferred life to those who were hurting. In every occurrence biblically listed, He healed everyone who came to Him.

Everything we understand about our relationship with God through Christ, we learned from Jesus' words and actions. We know that God loves us because Jesus said He does and showed us

He does. We know that we have grace because Jesus explained it and modeled grace in all that He did. We know that there is forgiveness from God because Jesus taught us about forgiveness and modeled that forgiveness. We know that God is not a God of judgment, wrath, and condemnation because Jesus modeled something much different. And we know that we have untapped potential to do all things through Christ and in authority over our enemy because that is what Jesus said and did. So if we accept at face value Christ's explanation about salvation, God's love, and grace, then why would we not follow suit when it comes to our authority on the earth?

If You've Seen Me, You've Seen the Father

I recently heard someone say, "Jesus Christ is perfect theology," and I agree wholeheartedly. When we look at the prophets and Old Testament depictions of God, we see a limited interpretation through the lenses of men who only knew God partially. But when we look at Jesus we see the offspring of God, carrying His DNA and sharing from the perspective of the Son of eternity who knew His Father intimately. And He says in John 14:7–9, "If you really know me, you will know my Father. . . . Anyone who has seen me has seen the Father."

If anyone knows the heart of God, it is His perfect Son. So when anyone depicts God in a way that does not look like Jesus (who mirrored the Father), their interpretation of who God is should be open to debate and questioned. Jesus said that He is the truth (John 14:6). So let everyone else be a liar.

Jesus said that the kingdom of God is at hand (Mark 1:15 NASB). That means it's present. It's here. It's not somewhere in the by and by. No, it is attainable in the here and now. That kingdom trumps every other king and kingdom.

Satan definitely has his own kingdom and representatives, but you serve the King of kings and the Lord of lords. At the name of Jesus, every other king bows his knee. This is why, when you know what your authority really is, then you understand that you don't have to live bound by any attack or lie of your enemy. Every demon in existence is subjected to the King who resides within you and whose kingdom you have complete authority to access and institute.

He Who Is in You Is Greater . . .

You can't give away what you don't have, but when Jesus said the kingdom of God is within you, it was so you would have the revelation that *you* carry that kingdom and authority every place you go with the ability to give it away (or in other words you have the ability to institute it and place a demand upon that kingdom power within wherever you are). Everywhere you go, people are hurting. Because you have the God of the universe within you, guiding you and empowering you with His authority, when you encounter hurting people you have the ability through prayer and your testimony of experiences to impart to them what God has given to you.

When the Bible says we are joint heirs with Christ, it means we draw from the same account and we carry the same Spirit of God and authority that Jesus did to institute the principles of the kingdom of heaven in every place we see hell on the earth.

Christian means "Christ Like" or "Little Christ." You are in covenant with and empowered by the same God who empowered and directed Jesus. The same kingdom at His disposal is at your disposal. The Bible says in reference to your authority over Satan, "The one who is in you is greater than the one who is in the world" (1 John 4:4).

To put it plainly, after all that Jesus said about who you are in Christ, if in your mind you don't think you can experience victory over the attacks of the Devil until you die, I have a question for you: Is it possible that maybe in your eyes, death is your savior instead of Jesus? I realize that statement is direct, but it is meant to inspire you to really consider what your actions or mind-sets reveal about what you believe.

When Jesus sat down at the right hand of the Father, the Holy Spirit was released to empower you with the same power that Jesus exhibited and walked in. Jesus didn't die and we weren't given the gift of the Holy Spirit of God residing within us to live a defeated and unfulfilled life.

It's Already in You

The Bible tells us that the fullness of the Godhead was in Jesus (Colossians 2:9–23), and just as He is, so are we in this world (1 John 4:17). You are empowered with limitless potential. Maybe it's because you were created for more than you have experienced or even believed was possible that the Bible says, "Seek first [God's] kingdom and his righteousness, and all these things will be given to you" (Matthew 6:33).

When you've had those thoughts and gut feelings about evil being prevalent in the world and how it just doesn't seem right to experience so much sin around you, based upon what you have been taught about God and His love, maybe you were right. Maybe it's not right that these things are happening.

What if what we have been taught about God and His love toward us is completely right, but what we been taught about God just *fixing* everything for us is not. What if He intended us to be in the world as His kingdom ambassadors, operating in His authority to make a difference in every environment that we step into? What if you've been waiting on God to do for you the very thing that He empowered you to do?

Maybe, just maybe, when Jesus said we could do even greater things than He did because He was going to the Father (John 14:12) and sending the Holy Spirit to live within us and empower us (v. 26, Acts 1:8, Ephesians 3:20), He actually meant what He said. And if He did, how might that influence your perceptions of *who God is* in light of this new revelation? What would it mean for *who you are* as a child of God in a loving relationship with Him? Would it give you a different perspective on the issues and who may be responsible for your experiences in the environments *where you have been*? What would this new perspective mean for *where you are now*, and ultimately your future experiences of *where you are going*?

You don't have to wait until eternity, after death, to experience the kingdom of God. The kingdom is at hand and within you!

Chapter 33

Keep on Knocking

I hope you are beginning to actually believe that maybe there is more for you to experience than what you have been taught or personally experienced. I believe your spirit is confirming in you that what you've been reading about who God says you are is actually the truth. I pray that your mind, will, and emotions are beginning to agree with God's Word about who you are really intended to be.

We stated in earlier chapters that without faith it's impossible to fully agree with God. After years in ministry and considering multiple angles for what faith actually is and looks like, at times I have found myself struggling with the concept of whether I was actually instituting faith or just simply living with hope. I wanted to make sure I was walking in faith and not just hope, because it seemed from the multiple scriptures I read that faith was the catalyst to experiencing the breakthroughs that often eluded me in my Christian walk, even as a pastor.

The problem was I didn't properly understand what hope actually was and how it was an essential aspect of releasing faith. To me *hope* was another word for a wish or distant desire that I wasn't sure would come to pass but sure *hoped* it would. As a result, when I read in Hebrews 11:1 that "faith is confidence in what we hope for," it didn't make sense to me. I felt conflicted because in my mind *faith* was something I extended because I *believed*. And *hope* felt more like a product of *unbelief* or perhaps what I resorted to when I didn't have enough faith. It was all very difficult for me to process.

However, in recent years I've discovered new information on the subject of hope that gave it the continuity it previously lacked, at least in my understanding. What I learned is that from a biblical perspective, hope is the joyful anticipation of something good happening. From this perspective, faith and hope are inseparable because faith in God empowers you to joyfully anticipate Him doing good in your life. This understanding completely lines up with the other scriptures referencing that without faith it's impossible to fully agree with God. It's also important to realize that any area where we do not feel hope (joyful anticipation of something good happening) in God and His promises may actually be under the mental influence of a lie (which as we discussed in previous chapters can also impact our experiential realities).

When we release faith, we acknowledge His Word and His promises; we place our agreement in who He says He is, who He says we are, and what He says He will do; and then we anticipate God fulfilling His Word in our lives. With this new understanding of hope, it caused me to revisit my thoughts and what I was taught about faith.

Faith and Formulas

As a teenager, I heard that if I prayed for something more than once, then I wasn't "walking in faith." Now, I'm a guy who likes formulas. I want A + B to = C because when it does, then it is replicable. So I did as I was told—I prayed and then just thanked God for the breakthrough. And I think, to a great extent, this formula has some relevance as it pertains to exhibiting faith. After all, if you *really* believe God is not deaf and when you pray He hears you, then asking once should be just fine. But I'm too cerebral, and when the answer didn't come in the timing that I expected, or in the way that I wanted, I slipped out of faith. I had no explanation for why things weren't happening and ultimately wondered if I had ever really had faith to begin with.

Then I read Matthew 7:7 in the Amplified Bible and I found myself confused as it seemed to contradict my faith formula:

Aaron D. Davis

Ask and keep on asking and it will be given to you; seek and keep on seeking and you will find; knock and keep on knocking and the door will be opened to you.

I had been in ministry for over twenty years before I found myself questioning this scripture and I asked God, "Which is it? Do I ask once and then just believe, or do I ask and keep on asking?" His answer surprised me when I heard Him say, "It's both."

For some, their faith is already developed to the point where when they ask God to meet their need, they just believe He will. But others aren't quite there yet. Then God showed me this next scenario as an example.

Imagine for a moment that I called you, told you I was home, and asked you to come to my house because I have a check for you that will pay off all your debt. When you get in the car to drive over, you are likely *hoping* (in both the traditional perspective of a *distant wish* and the biblical sense of a *joyful anticipation*) that I am going to do what I said I would do.

If you get to my house and knock on the door, you are likely still hoping I'm going to do what I said. When I don't answer the door immediately, doubt has a moment to set in. What you do after that point will indicate what you really believe about what I said. (As I've said many times now in this book, you don't have to tell me what you believe; your actions show me.)

If you turn and walk away after knocking a few times, your actions reveal that you had initially hoped I was going to be there and do what I said I was going to do, but at some point doubt and unbelief set in and kept you from continuing to exhibit faith.

Keep Knocking

We all reach that place where we question things. We all wonder sometimes if God hears the knocking. Keep knocking!

When doubt comes in, keep knocking.

When the voices in your head say God's promises must not be for you, keep knocking.

When your hand gets tired, keep knocking.

Keep on Knocking

*For we are not fighting against flesh-and-blood enemies,
but against evil rulers and authorities of the unseen world,
against mighty powers in this dark world,
and against evil spirits in the heavenly places.*
(Ephesians 6:12 NLT)

If God said it in His Word, He meant it. Sometimes there are things that are influencing our realities that we may not even be aware of. The Bible says that we war against "authorities the powers of this dark world and against the spiritual forces of evil in the heavenly realms" (Ephesians 6:12). We see an example of this in the life of Daniel (Daniel 10:13). He prayed for something, and twenty-one days later the angel of the Lord appeared and told him that the answer was sent immediately when he prayed, but the Prince of the kingdom of Persia (an authority of the unseen world) warred against the answer ever reaching Daniel and delayed it for those twenty-one days. During that time, Daniel kept praying. He kept knocking (if you will).

When you knock and keep on knocking, the repetition and tenacity not to quit allow you to continue placing your agreement in the Word of God and release faith into your circumstances. For some it may be the tenth knock; for another it might be the fiftieth knock. But at some point the intentionality not to quit causes you to step into faith by default as your actions say, "I believe You will do what You said You will do."

What it comes down to is this: God wants to give good gifts to His children. He wants for you to be free. Sometimes things take a bit longer than we would expect, like what happened with Daniel. The important thing is, whether you stand there waiting and believing or you keep on knocking, whatever you do, don't throw in the towel and give up.

God is faithful to finish what He has begun. The answer is on its way! He wants you to experience the limitless freedom, power, and potential that He created you for even more than you do. His promises are true. The check has been signed. Now keep knocking if necessary, and take possession of what He has promised.

Chapter 34

The Power of a Declaration

The Bible is the inspired Word of God. The word *inspired* means "breathed upon or God breathed." Placing your faith in agreement with God's Word has power, and one of the best ways to create or change an environment is to speak and pray scriptures and the promises of God that coincide with what you are experiencing or need to experience.

We talked in a previous chapter about how Jesus was our example and that He didn't cower in the face of demonic adversity. Matthew, Mark, and Luke describe an account where Jesus encountered the Devil face-to-face and was tempted by him.

The Temptation of Jesus
Then Jesus was led by the Spirit into the wilderness to be tempted there by the devil. For forty days and forty nights he fasted and became very hungry. During that time the devil came and said to him, "If you are the Son of God, tell these stones to become loaves of bread." But Jesus told him, "No! The Scriptures say, 'People do not live by bread alone, but by every word that comes from the mouth of God.'" Then the devil took him to the holy city, Jerusalem, to the highest point of the Temple, and said, "If you are the Son of God, jump off! For the Scriptures say, 'He will order his angels to protect you. And they will hold you up with their hands so you won't even hurt your foot on a stone.'" Jesus responded, "The Scriptures also say, 'You must not test the Lord your God.'" Next the devil took him to the peak of a very high mountain and showed him all the kingdoms of the world and

> *their glory. "I will give it all to you," he said, "if you will kneel down and worship me." "Get out of here, Satan," Jesus told him. "For the Scriptures say, 'You must worship the L<small>ORD</small> your God and serve only him.'" Then the devil went away, and angels came and took care of Jesus.*
> (Matthew 4:1–11 NLT)

In the face of this adversity, when His enemy was attempting to deceive Him into sinning, Jesus combated the Devil with the Word of God. When the Devil posed a temptation, Jesus quoted the Bible out loud in His own defense. At one point the Devil even attempted to manipulate Jesus with the Word of God when he said, "The Scriptures say that His angels will protect you."

Satan is a conniving adversary. He's strategic in his attacks. He will tell you what you want to hear and he'll hit you when you are down. The Bible wouldn't have called these *temptations* if they didn't actually tempt Jesus. He was hungry, He was weak, and He was facing the very adversary that He was sent to liberate mankind from. The Devil hit Jesus at His darkest moment, when He was separated from the support of others and He was hurting. Still, Jesus found strength in the declaration of God's Word. The Bible is the sword of the Spirit, and Jesus showed us in that moment how to use it against the one who comes to deceive, steal, kill, and destroy.

You've Got to Move Your Mouth if You're Gonna Move Your Mountain

We have been given the Bible so we can know God's thoughts regarding specific issues of life, but *declaring* the Word in order to be able to wield it as a weapon requires *knowing* that Word. This is why daily reading and studying the Bible is essential!

> *Consequently, faith comes from hearing the message, and the message is heard through the word about Christ.*
> (Romans 10:17)

The Bible is our instruction manual for discovering who God is, who we are, what His promises are, how He feels about us, and how He feels about what we are doing. Hearing the message of God through His Word and allowing it to build our faith is why it is also very important to intentionally place yourself in environments with other believers where your faith will be built.

So let's do it—full of belief, confident that we're presentable inside and out. Let's keep a firm grip on the promises that keep us going. He always keeps his word. Let's see how inventive we can be in encouraging love and helping out, not avoiding worshiping together as some do but spurring each other on.
(Hebrews 10:24–25 MSG)

Pastors and teachers have been called by God to help us grow in our faith. It's essential to read the Bible, but also hearing scriptures expounded on by people who have dedicated their lives to studying it and teaching it helps us grow all the more, and gives us the clarity necessary when it comes to wielding that sword of the Spirit through our own prayers and declarations.

I have hidden your word in my heart, that I might not sin against you.
(Psalm 119:11 NLT)

God's Word spoken through your mouth has creative and combative power! Jesus told us to *speak* to the mountain in faith if we want to see it move. I recently heard my friend Pastor Patrick Norris put it this way: "You've got to move your mouth if your gonna move your mountain," and I laughed at the simplicity, practicality, and truth of it. When the enemy comes against you, find the scriptures necessary to declare over your situation. They will give you the ability to triumph over any attacks of the enemy. If you feel afraid, declare:

For God did not give us a spirit of timidity or cowardice or fear, but [He has given us a spirit] of power and of love and of sound

judgment and personal discipline [abilities that result in a calm, well-balanced mind and self-control].
(2 Timothy 1:7 AMP)

If you feel lonely or unloved or defeated, declare:

Yet in all these things we are more than conquerors and gain an overwhelming victory through Him who loved us [so much that He died for us]. For I am convinced [and continue to be convinced—beyond any doubt] that neither death, nor life, nor angels, nor principalities, nor things present and threatening, nor things to come, nor powers, nor height, nor depth, nor any other created thing, will be able to separate us from the [unlimited] love of God, which is in Christ Jesus our Lord.
(Romans 8:37–39 AMP)

If you have been falsely accused, declare:

But the LORD is with me like a mighty warrior; so my persecutors will stumble and not prevail. They will fail and be thoroughly disgraced; their dishonor will never be forgotten.
(Jeremiah 20:11)

If you feel like you are too young to make a difference, declare:

But the LORD said to me, "Do not say, 'I am too young.' You must go to everyone I send you to and say whatever I command you. Do not be afraid of them, for I am with you and will rescue," declares the LORD. . . .
"Get yourself ready! Stand up and say to them whatever I command you. . . . They will fight against you but will not overcome you, for I am with you and will rescue you," declares the LORD.
(Jeremiah 1:7–8, 17, 19)

As we discussed in chapter 33, sometimes you have to knock and keep on knocking. The Bible says to declare a thing and it will be established, and sometimes your declaration can be a form of knocking and releasing faith.

    Declare and keep on declaring until that door opens. Move your mouth and speak to your mountain until that stronghold is defeated, or your experience mirrors what God promised you. Through your verbal declaration, you place your agreement in God's Word. Declare His promises and move those mountains out of your way by the power of the Word of God.

Chapter 35

It Is Finished

In John 19:30, as Jesus was taking His last breath on the cross, He declared, "It is finished!" In that moment, Jesus restored to mankind that which was lost. Up until that moment, man was separated from God by sin. We could only approach God through a priest. God only communicated to man through His chosen prophets. Our sin was only temporarily covered through the sacrifices performed by a priest. But Jesus became the final and perfect sacrifice for our sins. He restored the relationship that had been broken and reinstated the authority to implement God's kingdom on earth that man lost when he partnered with the kingdom of sin. Jesus restored man to the limitless freedom, power, and potential that he was created to live in when God created him in the first place.

It is because of Jesus that we have the authority to carry the kingdom of God into every arena that we see the kingdom of darkness reigning in the world. Because of this authority, sin only has the authority that we give it. You are no longer bound by sin. You are a child of God who has the potential to walk in the authority of the King of kings and the Lord of lords if you choose to. When you make a mistake it's not because you are powerless against sin; it's because you yielded your authority in that moment.

But you can take it back.

You can look that sin in the eyes and tell it *no*. You can tell that stronghold that has oppressed you and stolen from you your entire life that it must go. You can command the Devil to leave as you renounce the powers of darkness influencing your life due to invitation and intrusion.

> *But He gives us more and more grace [through the power of the Holy Spirit to defy sin and live an obedient life that reflects both our faith and our gratitude for our salvation].*
> *Therefore, it says, "God is opposed to the proud and haughty, but [continually] gives [the gift of] grace to the humble [who turn away from self-righteousness]." So submit to [the authority of] God. Resist the devil [stand firm against him] and he will flee from you. Come close to God [with a contrite heart] and He will come close to you.*
> (James 4:6–8 AMP)

The Devil has tried to convince you that you are not free. He has tried to manipulate the scriptures to make you feel condemned. He has told you that you gave him a right to be there. And he has tried to convince you that you don't have the power to stand against his temptation. The reason he does these things is because he doesn't want you to step into faith and abolish the strongholds he has placed in your life to keep you from reaching your God-ordained destiny.

Now that you have been given the insight into Satan's deceitful ways, when the enemy of your soul (mind, will, and emotions) comes against you, you must declare to him that you cancel the contract that sin gave him to influence your life. Remember the knowledge of the limitless potential that is placed in you. The sacrifice of Christ and your covenant with God cancels any of sin's former authority in your life. You are a new creation.

You have the mind of Christ and can access the very thoughts of God pertaining to your life and His will for your victory.

You have authority over all the works of the Devil!

You don't have to remain where you were yesterday.

You have experienced the limitless freedom, power, and potential that is found in the finished work of Christ!

What Do You See?

It Is Finished

See yourself today as the conqueror and inheritor of His promises that God has made you to be. If you can see it, you will be it. The same mind that was in Christ is in you. Focus your mind upon the promises of God.

Finally, believers, whatever is true, whatever is honorable and worthy of respect, whatever is right and confirmed by God's word, whatever is pure and wholesome, whatever is lovely and brings peace, whatever is admirable and of good repute; if there is any excellence, if there is anything worthy of praise, think continually on these things [center your mind on them, and implant them in your heart].
(Philippians 4:8 AMP)

The New Living Translation of this scripture says, "Fix your thoughts . . ." I love the word *fix* here because although in context it means to focus your mind, the word *fix* can also mean "to correct what is broken." Our broken thoughts and incorrect belief systems can be fixed as we center our minds, thoughts, prayers, declarations, and faith in agreement with the Word and promises of God.

You are who God says you are, and every day that you exercise that belief system you build your faith and abolish the strength of the stronghold that was rooted in wrong belief systems.

I opened this book with the scripture Isaiah 9:6–7, and I think it's worth repeating as we acknowledge how far we've come, and the One who has brought us to this point.

For to us a child is born, to us a son is given, and the government will be on his shoulders. And he will be called Wonderful Counselor, Mighty God, Everlasting Father, Prince of Peace. Of the greatness of his government and peace there will be no end. He will reign on David's throne and over his kingdom, establishing and upholding it with justice and righteousness from that time on and forever. The zeal of the LORD Almighty will accomplish this.

This was a prophecy of the birth of Jesus by the prophet Isaiah some seven hundred years before the birth of Christ. In this text Isaiah says, "The government will be on his shoulders . . . of the greatness of his government . . . there will be no end."

This entire scripture is referring to the reestablishment of the kingdom of God and the authority to govern (government) of that kingdom in the earth being given to us through Jesus. I love the words, "Of the greatness [or immensity of impact] of his government [authority to govern] . . . there will be no end [no limits, *limitless*]."

Jesus declared, "I am the light of the world" (John 8:12), but He went on to say that He was delegating that authority to you and that now you are the light of the world (Matthew 5:14–16).

You are not only a recipient of freedom; you are an ambassador of it! You are created to take what you have learned and implemented and to become an instrument of liberty for others who may also be in captivity like you once were. You've heard it said that hurt people hurt people, but I'm more convinced than ever that healed people heal people and free people free people!

In Jesus' final moments on earth, He looked at His disciples and told them that all the authority in heaven and earth had been given to Him and He was giving it to them. He went on to instruct them to take the limitless freedom, power, and potential that He had purchased for them (and modeled before them) and implement it to do even greater things than He did in His lifetime.

Jesus has provided you with the same ability as the disciples to access the *limitless* that the kingdom of God supplies. The same Holy Spirit poured out on the disciples resides within and empowers you!

Believers around the world are hearing teachings like those presented by Jesus in the Bible (and reiterated in this book) and are coming to new levels of understanding regarding who God is, what Christ really did for them, and who they really are intended to be as ambassadors of His kingdom. They are bringing the light of God's love and power to any place where they see darkness in the world.

You've begun down the road to experiencing this limitless freedom, power, and potential in your life. Understand that these

It Is Finished

blessings will not come without opposition from your enemy. After all, he has spent much effort and time attempting to keep you in the dark and in bondage. But remember, He who is in you is greater than he who is in the world. Jesus paid a great price for you to have this limitless freedom, and God wants you to experience it. God has begun a good work in you, and He is faithful to complete it.

You are far more than just another person who has made mistakes or sinned. You are a child of God; an ambassador of Christ, commissioned to fulfill His desires on the earth; and a carrier of the same Spirit and authority that empowered Jesus to completely rock the world. Embrace the truth of all God has created you to be. Place your agreement in that truth. Extend your faith and declarations toward that truth, and watch the mountains that were previously insurmountable obstacles melt like wax in the presence of the God who empowers you. They will no longer keep you from your destiny.

Age does not limit your authority, nor does gender, race, social status, or ability. You are who God says you are. You can be who He created you to be. You can experience today the freedom, power, and potential you were created for.

See it!
Believe it!
Be it!

You are embarking on a new chapter in your life. The lenses are clearer than they have ever been. The blinders are off. And the possibilities are limitless.

Now to Him who is able to [carry out His purpose and] do superabundantly more than all that we dare ask or think [infinitely beyond our greatest prayers, hopes, or dreams], according to His power that is at work within us, to Him be the glory in the church and in Christ Jesus throughout all generations forever and ever.
Amen.
(Ephesians 3:20–21 AMP)

Conclusion

I hope you enjoyed *Limitless Young Adults: You Can Experience the Freedom, Power & Potential You Were Created For*. As one who struggled with the bondage of strongholds from my childhood well into my adult life, I wrote this book to provide the type of information I wish I had twenty years ago. I've included practical applications for overcoming the beliefs that are responsible for holding back millions of Christian teenagers and young adults around the world from being all of who God created them to be.

As a young minister in my twenties, I was aware that I needed to experience more in the freedom and power department, but I didn't believe I was a good fit to enroll in a weekend-long intensive deliverance session in order to experience it (and at the time, that was all that was available to me). In my mind, the people who went to the weekend retreats were dealing with problems much deeper than mine (not to mention, I was a pastor and didn't want people to know some of the things I was secretly warring with). I understand now that this perception is flawed and that I would have likely benefited from the experience. But that was nevertheless my perception at the time.

In releasing *Limitless Young Adults*, my desire is to provide the information about the progression of strongholds and the elimination of them that years of research and experience have given me insight into. What I have come to understand is there is a very broad demographic of teenagers and young adults who, like I did, have struggled with the same two or three strongholds that have repeatedly placed a ceiling on their success and capped their potential. And many who would like to experience freedom have not been taught the necessary information and means to become as free as Jesus intended for them to be.

Conclusion

The truth contained in *Limitless Young Adults* has the potential to completely transform your world. I've been teaching this material for years now, and when applied, I've seen countless numbers of people set free from the strongholds that have held them back their entire lives.

It's not that these strongholds never have the potential to come back. And it should be obvious that our lives present a great soil for them to grow in. However, after being enlightened to the truth of God's Word and directly addressing these strongholds by redirecting your agreement and aligning your faith and declaration with God's Word, when they do attempt to come back, you have the ability to recognize them in seedling form and have the tools to pull them up before they ever take root again.

Now that you're able to recognize these strongholds for what they are and how they've impacted your existence, you may desire to continue to pursue a deeper understanding of living in the limitless freedom, power, and potential that God has provided for you. For those who would like to take their learning and experience to the next level, I have created the company *Limitless Solutions* to provide multiple additional resources including books, small-group curriculums, one-on-one and group coaching, *Limitless* Breakthrough Seminars, and training for churches/nonprofits to teach and institute *Limitless* as a curriculum and host their own Breakthrough seminars.

Some of these resources are outlined on the following pages, but my website will provide continually updated information available to you as our team endeavors to expand our *Limitless* library of resources at www.LimitlessSolutions.org.

Along with education, mentoring, and coaching, I believe wholeheartedly that having a connection to a local church is a vital part of spiritual growth, but many people do not know which church in their area will provide them with what they are looking for. As a result, I have provided a link on my website with a list of churches around the world who have a passion for the *Limitless* experience. This list will continue to grow as we are made aware of more churches. If your church is one of those churches and would like to be included on this list, please contact me.

Aaron D. Davis

    Thank you for taking the time to read *Limitless Young Adults: You Can Experience the Freedom, Power, and Potential You Were Created For*. If you have any questions or comments, I would love to hear from you so please feel free to e-mail me to let me know how this book or any of my other resources have impacted you. And don't forget to go online and leave a review of this book on Amazon.com or your favorite bookseller's website.

About the Author

Aaron Davis, also known as the Tattooed Preacher (www.TattooPreacher.com), has been an ordained minister for over twenty years. This is his fifth book, following *The Spirit of Religion* (2006), *Love Thy Neighbor* (2006), best-selling *Quantum Christianity: Believe Again* (2015), and Limitless (2016).

Aaron has served in ministry as a youth pastor, an associate pastor, a traveling evangelist, a street evangelist, a church elder, an online technology pastor, a worship pastor, a freedom/deliverance ministries pastor, and has served on the board of trustees in one of the most respected ministries in the United States. He has worked with and ministered to the homeless, inner-city youth, gang members, and drug addicts. He has had multiple opportunities to work privately in a mentoring and service capacity with celebrities, their families, and their staff.

He travels internationally as a keynote speaker on the subjects of leadership and team development, referencing his extensive leadership experience in many arenas including law enforcement, SWAT, conflict resolution, crisis emergency plan development, being a man, husband, and father, and experiencing personal freedom, in both corporate and faith-based seminars and workshops.

Most recently, Aaron launched the new website www.LimitlessSolutions.org for the growing library of resources related to this book, including video coaching, personal coaching, curriculum implementation, freedom coach training, and ministry staff development. He is extending the *Limitless* name and principles into corporate training and coaching as well.

Aaron was a law enforcement officer from 1999 until 2008, serving as a DARE officer, a school resource officer, a detective sergeant (criminal investigations division), and a SWAT team member, and was awarded Officer of the Year in 2002. An attempt was made on his life in the line of duty, forcing a medical retirement.

Aaron is originally from Detroit, Michigan, and lives with his wife of twenty years, Lisa, and his son, Rocky, in Nashville, Tennessee.

When he's not researching, writing, speaking in leadership events, coaching, and serving others, Aaron enjoys riding his Harley-Davidson motorcycle, scuba diving, skateboarding with Rocky, and being an intentional husband and father.

Contact Aaron:Aaron@LimitlessSolutions.org

If you enjoyed *Limitless: You Can Experience the Freedom Power and Potential You Were Created For,* and would like to read more content dedicated to deeply exploring the topics of the authority of the believer, what our covenant with God through Christ entails, and the power of the Kingdom of God residing within us, while also comparing the science backing the theology presented, order your copy of Aaron D. Davis' best-selling book, *Quantum Christianity: Discovering the Science of Scripture. Uncovering the Mysteries of Faith,* in print, digital, and audiobook (narrated by the author) versions today at: www.LimitlessSolutions.org, Amazon.com, or your favorite bookseller.

Why Coaching?

History reveals that if you continue to do what you have always done, you will get what you have always gotten. Without change, your circumstances will continue to be what they have always been, and coaching can help provide necessary insight into what those changes might look like for your life.

Some people will read *Limitless: You Can Experience the Freedom, Power and Potential You Were Created For* and be content to archive what they've learned and move on. Others will feel the desire to continue to pursue a deeper understanding of what experiencing freedom might mean for them.

You may want to pursue coaching if you feel any of these apply to you:

- You're tired of experiencing cycles of dissatisfaction and are determined to identify and change the things that have stifled your progress, robbed you of happiness, and kept you from experiencing your God-ordained destiny.
- You would like open and honest feedback, encouragement, and insight into some areas that may continue to create obstacles between where you are and where you want to be in life.
- You desire intentional accountability and clarity as you pursue the freedom, power, and potential you were created by God to experience.
- You are not connected with a church or ministry that has an intentional Freedom ministry.

At LimitlessSolutions.org we offer several options for coaching and training to meet every person where they are, and offer them additional tools to help them experience freedom. From one-on-one personal mentoring, to video coaching, to online group classes, the options continue to grow as the Limitless Solutions team grows and evolves.

One-On-One Mentoring

Everyone's experiences are different and that's why Aaron Davis and the Limitless Solutions coaches listen to what you need, evaluate possible pitfalls, help you set and discover paths to reach your goals, provide structure to support and offer you guidance throughout the process of overcoming strongholds in your life, and ultimately help you see what will be necessary to reach the place of experiencing the meaningful victory that you desire for your life.

Note: Aaron will be personally taking on a select number of coaching clients a month and the coaching team will be available to continue to meet the needs of all additional clients.

For options and availability, see our website for more information: www.LimitlessSolutions.org.

Video Coaching and Online Group Classes

The vision for this type of coaching is a continued evolution between options of live group classes (with question and answer segments taking place with our coaches) and downloadable content-based video coaching sessions.

See our website for up-to-date available coaching and online class options.

Ministry Team Coaching and Curriculum Implementation

When hearing about the success of the *Limitless* classes and *Freedom* weekends that Aaron has developed and conducted, many pastors and leaders have asked him if there was any way they could implement the program for their church or ministry.

As a result, Aaron has created an entire *Limitless* curriculum and *Limitless Young Adults* curriculum for ministries, complete with digital book licensing, classroom/small group instructor's manual, student workbooks, classroom videos, a fully scripted *Freedom From Strongholds* weekend ministry experience, and more.

In order to help churches that may need additional information on how to implement the curriculum or would like guidance when conducting their own *Freedom* weekend experience, Aaron has made himself available as a consultant for your staff, and is available to facilitate a private *Freedom from Strongholds* weekend experience for your team or ministry in person.

Experiencing freedom from strongholds is a reality for your church, your staff, or your ministry and the *Limitless/Limitless Young Adults* curriculum can be an impacting tool to help empower your people to enter their tomorrow without carrying the weight of yesterday.

For questions and up-to-date information on available coaches, personal coaching options, staff coaching options, and curriculum implementation, visit www.LimitlessSolutions.org.

www.ingramcontent.com/pod-product-compliance
Lightning Source LLC
Chambersburg PA
CBHW070615300426
44113CB00010B/1532